The Baby Name Wizard

The Complete Book of Baby Names for Girls and Boys - Meaning, Origin, and Uniqueness

Table of Contents

Introduction

Finding a name for your baby can be a long and frustrating process. There are so many things to think about and so little time. Why can't the name just fall out of the sky or be given by God as it is in some movies? If only there was a simple way of finding the perfect name for my baby.

If this thought has crossed your mind, worry no more! With the help of this book, we doubt that you will have any difficulty with regards to finding the perfect name. In this book, you will find thousands of names with meaning and origin. Some you will adore, and some you will not, but see this process of searching as a gold miner does. You have to cut through some stone in order to get to the gold.

At the end of the book, you will get a checklist so you can test to see if you have found the right one.

So, without further ado, shall we get started?

Chapter 1

What's in a Name?

Deciding what to name your child is one of the most difficult and most important decisions you may ever make. After all, it sets the tone for his or her life! This guide will take you to step by step through the process of choosing a baby name, from what to avoid to what's trending.

Choosing the Perfect Name

Unfortunately, there's no one-size-fits-all formula for choosing the perfect baby name. A lot of the process depends on your preferences, traditions, and expectations. If you go into the baby naming process knowing you want a two-syllable girl's name that starts with an "S", this process will likely go a lot faster than if you were waiting to be surprised with the gender and are going into the process with no parameters.

Lucky for you, regardless of where you're at in the process, we've got you covered. Even if you think you already know what you want to name your son or daughter, there's no harm in making sure you don't make a mistake you might not even realize is a mistake. If you're certain about a name, make sure it follows all the things you should keep in mind, avoids any pitfalls, and falls in line with the final checklist. This guide is here to help you narrow your focus and avoid making a name mistake that will stay with your child for the rest of his or her life. We're here to make sure you choose the perfect name!

What to Keep in Mind When Choosing Your Baby's Name

The Popularity Factor

It happens... we hear a name we like on a TV show, or at the playground, or in a restaurant. It's easy to get stuck on a name and decide that that's the name your child is going to have, but do your research first. If you heard the name, that means at least one other person in your area has the name. There's a chance it could be a unique name you just happened to overhear, or it could be one of the most popular baby names this year.

Names like Ava and Emma are adorable, but your daughter is bound to have two neighbors named Ava and four friends at her daycare named Emma, so you might want to think twice before giving your child a popular name. Noah has topped the list of popular boys' names for the past four years. Unless you want your son to share his name with thousands of others his age, opt against Noah until the popularity fades a bit.

Studies have even been done that found that nearly half of the parents who regret the name they gave their child feel that way because the name got way too popular. Do some research and ask a few close friends—especially those with young kids in daycare and school— their thoughts. If this is your first child, or you haven't had children in the past three or five years, you might be out of touch with the current trends. Names that were popular when you were a kid are likely old news now, and names that you might think are unique could be topping all the baby name lists.

How Has It Been Used?

While naming after pop culture characters and celebrities is very on-trend right now (more about that later), consider how ordinary names are used in pop culture before deciding on those names for your child. For example, you may love the name Miley for a girl, but know that she will undoubtedly be asked at least once a week for the rest of her life if she's named after Miley Cyrus. If you're crazy about the name Stephanie but are looking for a unique spelling and opt for Stefani, you will constantly be asked if you're a big Gwen Stefani fan.

Along the same lines, you certainly don't want to choose a name that is associated with negativity. Obvious examples include Adolf, Osama, Ted, or any "O" name with a middle name or prefix that would result in them being called "OJ". You might want to go so far as to not naming after any fictional villains, like Lord Voldemort from the Harry Potter series or Cruella deVil from 101 Dalmatians.

Potential Nicknames

You certainly don't want to choose a name that just has a bunch of awful puns or rhymes waiting around the corner. We've all been through middle school and high school and know how cruel kids can be. Consider any possible nicknames or rhymes that can develop from the name you like to ensure that other children don't have a nice laugh at the expense of your child's name.

For example, the name Chuck rhymes with some words that aren't so nice and you probably wouldn't want other kids using in reference to your child. There's also Fatty Patty, Harry who's Hairy, Icky Vicky, Smelleanor, Elliott... the list goes on! Go through the alphabet and make sure the name(s) you like don't have any unfortunate rhymes, and take to the internet to do a quick search on whether or not there are any not-so-great nicknames for your chosen name(s).

Pronunciation is Key

Let's not beat around the bush. To go along with refraining from giving your child a name that is completely unheard of or ridiculous, don't give your child a name that is difficult to pronounce. Sure, there are people everywhere that can mispronounce names as simple as Michael or Kristin, but don't make it any harder on your child than it has to be. If their name is pronounced as Kylie, there is no need to spell it Khileighe. If you want a unique spelling, maybe go for something that is different from the normal Kylie but still can be read without missing a beat, like Kiley or Kyleigh.

This is something that can impact your child from the time they're born until they're in their sixties and beyond. It's simple: have some people read the name as you want to spell it, and make sure that at least 90% of them read it correctly at first glance. If you're set on giving your child a unique name that no one else has, by no means, go for it! Please just make sure it's easily pronounceable.

We don't mean to scare you if the name you love is just a bit different, because what we're talking about are simply absurd spelling and made-up names. Let's take a look at some of the names we're talking about:

- Maaike
- Kyler
- Saoirse
- Chiwetel
- Ioan
- Anais
- Maureen
- Kaia

If you're set on a name like Siobhan, Schuyler, or Isla, you'll also have to accept the fact that you and your child will be subject to answering pronunciation questions at least once a day for the rest of your/their lives.

Remember That They Grow Up

This is a big one that not a lot of parents think about. Sure, a six-month-old girl named Charlie or Lily is cute, but what about a 40-year-old with the same name? When naming a child, most people don't think about how the name will impact them for years to come, but it's a name they're stuck with forever. Picture them in high school, college, and beyond. If you would be embarrassed to have a name at any of those ages, you probably shouldn't make your child endure it.

Nicknames are the best solution to this problem. Instead of naming your son Johnny, name him Jonathan and simply call him Johnny when he's young. As he gets older, he can decide what he wants to be called. You can always use nicknames that change with age, so consider going with Charlotte and calling her Charlie when she's young, then switching to Charlotte as she gets older. If you give your child a name like Ellie, Davey, or Izzy, they're stuck with the name as they get older, so consider that before opting for a name because it's "cute"!

Adventures in Baby Naming

The name is the first gift you will give to your bundle of joy, and picking the right name is almost certainly one of the most important decisions you can make before the big day arrives.

How to choose a name can be both a challenging and stressful task for parents. A name that you feel comfortable saying and a name that your child will be proud of throughout his/her life are just a few of the many considerations when choosing a name. With an overwhelming number of options to choose from, picking that perfect name for your child may seem difficult.

Whether you are looking for a unique name for your child or you want something meaningful, this book offers an excellent selection of baby names for boys and girls including their meanings.

The process of pregnancy, getting everything ready for the big day, and deciding what you are going to name your baby can sometimes feel like a chore to fit in your already jam-packed schedule. So to make the task of choosing a nameless stressful, the following are some ideas that you can try:

1. Jot down all the names you have in mind. You can also ask your family and friends to contribute a possible name for the baby.
2. Announce it. Tell all your friends and family members that you are looking for that perfect name for your baby and that their suggestions would be very much appreciated.
3. Narrow down your choices. Pick at least five names that sound good when you say them. Write each one on a card and read them out every day for a week. You will see that at the end of the week, one will probably become your favorite.

4. Along with this book, you can leaf through magazines and even phone books to see if there are names that sound good to you.
5. Practice saying different names loudly and several times in a row. Then ask family members which ones they like best.
6. Read through the following names of boys and girls in this book, and note down your favorites!

When beginning the baby-naming process, don't be overwhelmed. Try to have fun and don't be stressed. Plan a get-together with a group of friends over dinner or coffee to talk through ideas. Have a date night with your spouse, partner, or S.O. and begin an informal discussion about names you like. If you already know the sex of your baby, cut the task time in half, since you will only have to focus on either male or female names. Maybe you're even one of the lucky ones who've already had a few names picked out long before you got the news that you were expecting. You may have plenty of time to make this decision, so take it at a comfortable pace and enjoy the adventure.

Tips for Choosing a Good Name

When you come up with a preliminary list of names you like, ask yourself the following questions about each name:

- Does it have a positive association for you or remind you of someone you like and respect?
- Is it compatible with your last name?
- Does it feel fresh or timeless?
- If heritage matters, does it reflect your family's culture?
- Does it have a definition that feels suitable?
- Will others respond well to the name?
- Is it easy to spell, easy to pronounce, and easy to remember?

- Do you like the initials the full name creates?
- Will it lend itself to a cute and kind nickname?
- Will the name stand the test of time and sound as good to you in thirty years as it does today?

If you can't narrow down your names to one favorite, consider turning one into a middle name. Or create a middle name from the mother's maiden name. As a final thought, once you narrow down your top few choices, take a few days to see if you are as enthusiastic about your choice tomorrow as you are today.

Baby Name "Don'ts"

On the other side of the spectrum, here are a few things NOT to do when deciding on your baby's name:

Don't choose a name that other kids are apt to pick on. Some kids can be cruel, and you want to protect your child from others' ignorance.

Don't get too trendy. Britney is cute today, but how will "Nana Britney" sound?

Don't pick a name that rhymes with anything bad or sounds too similar to a word that is negative, obscene, or too slangy.

Don't go to the extreme with alternative spellings. A unique spelling makes a common name more distinctive, but you're also guaranteed that you and your child will always have to spell it out to others.

Don't choose a name that when coupled with your last name forms the name of someone famous (like "George Clooney" or "Katy Perry"), because those comparisons will be made for a lifetime.

Don't pick a name that sounds like it would be better suited for a pet. Fifi, Smokey, and Misty are cute for dogs and cats ... not so cute for kids.

Don't let choosing a name to create a rift between you and your partner. The process should be unifying, not divisive.

Don't tell too many people about the name you selected until it's on the birth certificate. Everyone has an opinion, and you're sure to hear it. Yours is the only one that counts.

Puzzles

Some people just prefer to keep the names from the family, or give them a "rearrangement" to contain more names or the same letters. Depends on what the parents wish in this direction; some parents combine part or all of their first names to create a name for their child. Of course, not every set of names lends itself to this trick but when it works, it's quite amazing.

Spontaneity

This interesting and very used method of choosing a name finds its use especially when time is short and the parents just don't seem to reach a final agreement regarding the name. It can come to you at your workplace, when driving or listening to the radio, when talking to someone or during any activity. It has no rules, just appears like a Eureka moment and can impress you so much that it makes you adopt him forever. The story behind the name is also a funny thing to remember and tell your baby about when he will ask how did you think about his name.

Stealing names

We are not suggesting that you steal your sister's favorite baby name right out from under her pregnant nose but statistics say that a surprising number of people do steal baby names! Pay attention around you and leave your ears open to any suggestions, even from other future parents. There have been many complaints about names that have been "stolen" but the reality is that once a name gets to be liked especially by a pregnant mother like you, or a responsible father looking for a baby name, there is no way you can convince anyone to give up and look for another. And nobody wants to upset a pregnant woman or a euphoric father!

Family and heritage

Family might drive you crazy when it comes to the name of your baby. Depending on the type of family (rich, aristocratic, independent or authoritarian), they might want to include a name from the family's lineage in your baby's name. Your child's heritage has importance if you want to accept it, and the solution can be found in accepting two names instead of one or to be flexible and modify slightly the names when necessary. Some say that it is recommended to continue the line of a certain family tradition in order to have the child protected and receive its well-deserved place in the family. Either way, it's advisable to consult family members especially if they have an important role in your baby's life. What is Meaning?

No one is likely to treat your daughter or son differently because their name means "hero" or "warrior" but the derivation of your baby's name is something you may want to think about. Especially if you are one of those people who care about symbols and meanings to everything in general. Depending on your language and culture, every name has a significance given by the religion, history or the word itself. You can name your child after a known leader or king (Attila, Franklin, Diana, Ludovic) or whatever you feel like, a color (Purple), a precious stone (Esmeralda) or some innovative combination (Isamar), but most probably people, including your child someday, will want to know what it means. This meaning gives not only a rational (or irrational explanation), but also a certain weight to your baby's personality. Each name carries energy derived from the vibration of the sound and also from it's more believed history. Everyone thinks of a particular personality when hearing "Lola", "Agatha", "Benjamin" or "Carmen". Pick your name and search its meaning, it will reflect maybe your expectations towards your child's life and character.

Anticipating nicknames

A nickname is so usual nowadays that it is advisable to think of it before you decide a name. Especially kids can be cruel when it comes to inventing a reason to laugh or mock someone, so try to anticipate any potentially embarrassing ones. The chances that you won't think of all the possibilities are obvious, but remember that nicknames are a passing period and won't stick forever. They will be invented or associated with some particularity of the child even if it has nothing to do with the name. Your duty is just to check for weird or ugly nicknames that could derive from your chosen name.

Initials

Especially when your baby has two names, the recommendation is to check how they sound together. Of course, if you already picked a perfect name and the initials are not so perfect then stick with the names, nothing else is important. Initials are not so commonly used and the best thing for everyone including your child is to pronounce the name entirely, not pieces, nicknames, initials or inventions. You know, of course, that is not truly possible when you involve your feelings and use diminutives to spoil and show tenderness. So going from Miguel to Miguelito or from Christina to Christy it's almost as natural as your real baby name.

Chapter 2

Boy and Girl Names with Meaning and Origin

Boy Names

Name	Meaning	origin
Aaden	little fiery one	American, Irish
Aarav	peaceful	Hindi
Aaron	high mountain; exalted	Hebrew
Aarush	first ray of sun	Hindi
Abdiel	servant of God	Hebrew
Abdullah	servant of Allah	Arabic
Abel	breath	Hebrew
Abraham	father of multitudes	Hebrew
Abram	high father	Hebrew
Ace	unity	Latin
Achilles	thin-lipped	Greek
Adam	son of the red earth	Hebrew
Adan	son of the red earth	Spanish
Aden	little and fiery	Irish
Adonis	lord	Greek
Adrian	man of Adria	Latin
Adriel	God is my master	Hebrew

Adrien	from Adria	French
Agustin	the exalted one	Latin
Ahmad	greatly praised	Arabic
Ahmed	greatly praised	Arabic
Aidan	little and fiery	Irish
Aiden	little and fiery	Irish
Alan	handsome; cheerful	Irish
Albert	noble; bright	German
Alberto	noble; bright	Germanic
Alden	old wise friend	English
Aldo	old and wise	Italian, German
Alec	defending men	Greek
Alejandro	defending men	Spanish
Alessandro	defending men	Italian
Alex	defending men	Greek
Alexander	defending men	Greek
Alexis	defender	Greek
Alexzander	defending men	Greek
Alfonso	noble; ready	Spanish, Italian
Alfred	wise counselor	English
Alfredo	wise counselor	Celtic
Ali	supreme; exalted	Arabic
Alijah	the Lord is my God	Hebrew
Allan	handsome; cheerful	Irish
Allen	handsome	Celtic
Alonso	"Adalfuns"	Portuguese, Spanish
Alonzo	noble; ready	Italian
Alvaro	cautious	Spanish
Alvin	noble friend	English
Amare	handsome	African
Amari	eternal	Hebrew
Ameer	king; treetop	Arabic, Hebrew

Name	Meaning	Origin
Amir	king; treetop	Arabic, Hebrew
Amos	carried by God	Hebrew
Anakin	warrior	American
Anders	strong and manly	Scandinavian
Anderson	son of Anders	Scandinavian
Andre	man	French, Portuguese
Andres	manly	Spanish
Andrew	strong and manly	Greek
Andy	strong and manly	Greek
Angel	messenger	Greek
Angelo	messenger	Italian
Anson	son of Anne	English
Anthony	priceless one	Latin
Antoine	priceless one	French
Anton	priceless one	German, Scandinavian
Antonio	priceless one	Spanish, Italian
Apollo	manly beauty	Greek
Archer	bowman	English
Ares	ruin; bane	Greek
Ari	lion of God	Hebrew
Arian	warrior; honourable	Indo-Iranian
Ariel	lion of God	Hebrew
Arjun	bright; shining; white	Hindi
Arlo	barberry tree	Spanish
Armando	soldier	Spanish
Portuguese	Italian	
Armani	freeman	Persian
Aron	enlightened; high mountain	Hebrew, Spanish
Arthur	bear	Celtic

17

Arturo	bear	Celtic
Aryan	warrior	Indo-Iranian
Asa	born in the morning	Hebrew
Asher	fortunate; happy one	Hebrew
Ashton	ash trees place	English
Atlas	a titan	Greek
Atticus	from Attica	Latin
August	great; magnificent	German
Augustine	great; magnificent	English
Augustus	great; magnificent	Latin
Austin	great; magnificent	English
Avery	ruler of the elves	English
Avi	father	Hebrew
Axel	father of peace	German
Axl	father of peace	Scandinavian
Axton	sword stone	English
Ayaan	God's gift	Arabic
Aydan	little fiery one	Irish
Ayden	little fiery one	Irish
Aydin	intelligent	Turkish
Azariah	helped by God	Hebrew
Barrett	bear strength	German
Baylor	one who delivers goods	English
Beau	handsome	French
Beckett	bee cottage	English, Irish
Beckham	homestead by the stream	English
Ben	son of	Hebrew
Benjamin	son of the right hand	Hebrew
Bennett	blessed	English
Benson	son of Ben	English
Bentlee	meadow with coarse grass	English
Bentley	meadow with coarse grass	English
Benton	bent grass enclosure	English

Billy	resolute protection	English
Bishop	overseer	English
Blaine	slender	Irish
Blaise	to lisp; stammer	French
Blake	fair-haired; dark	English
Blaze	one who stutters	Latin
Bo	to live	Swedish, Danish
Bobby	bright fame	English
Bode	shelter	Scandinavian
Boden	blonde; floor	Celtic, German
Bodhi	awakened	Sanskrit
Bodie	shelter; one who brings news	Scandinavian
Boone	a blessing	French
Boston	a place name	English
Bowen	son of Owen	Celtic
Braden	from Bradden, dweller near the broad valley	English
Bradley	dweller at the broad road	English
Brady	spirited	Irish
Braeden	broad and wide	Celtic
Braiden	broad valley	English
Brandon	from the beacon hill	English
Branson	sword	Germanic
Brantlee	fiery torch	English
Brantley	fiery torch	English
Braxton	Brock's settlement	English
Brayan	noble and virtuous	American, Celtic
Brayden	broad	English
Braydon	broad	English
Braylen	from the name Braydon and Lyn	American

Braylon	from the name Braydon and Lyn	American
Brecken	little freckled one	Irish
Brendan	prince	Irish
Brenden	prince	Irish
Brennan	brave	Gaelic
Brent	high place	English
Brentley	hilltop	Celtic
Brett	a native of France or England	English
Brian	strong and virtuous	Irish
Briar	a thorny patch	Word name
Brice	freckled	Scottish
Briggs	from the village near a bridge	English
Brixton	Brixton district of London	English
Brock	badger	English
Brodie	little ridge	Scottish
Brody	ditch	Scottish
Bronson	son of brown-haired one	English
Brooks	of the brook	English
Bruce	from the brushwood thicket	Scottish, English
Bruno	brown	German
Bryan	strong and virtuous	Irish
Bryant	strong and virtuous	Irish
Bryce	freckled	Scottish
Brycen	son of Brice	English
Bryson	son of Brice	English
Byron	barn for cows	English
Cade	round; barrel	English

Caden	companion of friend; warrior	Arabic, English
Caiden	fighter	Gaelic
Cain	spear; possessed	Hebrew
Cairo	victorious	Arabic
Caleb	devotion to God	Hebrew
Callan	battle; rock	Gaelic
Callen	rock	Gaelic
Callum	dove	Scottish, Latin
Calvin	hairless	Latin
Camden	winding valley	Scottish
Camdyn	winding valley	Scottish
Cameron	crooked nose	Scottish
Camilo	young ceremonial attendant	Latin
Camren	crooked nose	Scottish
Camron	crooked nose	Scottish
Canaan	merchant	Hebrew
Cannon	clergyman	English
Carl	free man	German
Carlos	free man	Spanish
Carmelo	cultivated terrain	Spanish
Carter	transporter of goods by cart	English
Case	observant	Irish
Casen	descendant of cathasach; pure	Irish, Scandinavian
Casey	brave in battle	Irish
Cash	wealthy man	English
Cason	descendant of cathasach; pure	Scandinavian, Irish

Cassius	hollow	Latin
Castiel	my cover is God	Hebrew
Cayden	fighter	Gaelic
Cayson	courageous and tough	Irish
Cedric	bounty	Celtic
Cesar	long haired Spanish	Latin
Chace	huntsman	English
Chad	protector	English
Chaim	life	Hebrew
Chance	good luck	English
Chandler	candle maker	French
Channing	young wolf	English
Charles	free man	French
Charlie	free man	English
Chase	dweller of the hunting ground	English
Chevy	knight	French
Chris	carrier of Christ	Greek
Christian	follower of Christ	Greek
Christopher	carrier of Christ	Greek
Clark	scribe	English
Clay	mortal	Teutonic
Clayton	mortal	English
Clyde	from the name of Scottish Clyde river	Scottish
Cody	helpful	Irish
Coen	bold advisor	Dutch
Cohen	priest	Hebrew
Colby	from the dark village	American
Cole	swarthy coal black	English
Coleman	dove	Irish
Colin	young pup	Scottis, Irish
Collin	young pup	Scottish, Irish

Colt	from the dark town	English
Colten	coal town	English
Colton	from the dark town	English
Conner	much desire	Irish
Connor	strong willed	Irish
Conor	lover of hounds	Irish
Conrad	brave counsel	German
Cooper	barrel maker	English
Corbin	raven	Latin
Corey	seething pool	Scottish
Cory	seething pool	Scottish
Craig	dwells at the crag	Scottish
Crew	dam-like structure	Welsh
Cristian	follower of Christ	Spanish
Cristiano	follower of Christ	Italian, Portoguese
Cristopher	bearer of Christ	Greek
Crosby	village with crosses	Irish
Cruz	cross	Portuguese
Cullen	handsome	Gaelic
Curtis	courteous	French
Cyrus	throne	Persian
Dakota	friend	Native American
Dallas	wise	Gaelic
Dalton	the settlement in the valley	English
Damari	gentle	Latin
Damian	to tame	Greek
Damien	one who tames	French
Damon	gentle	Greek
Dane	brook	English
Dangelo	from the angel	Italian
Daniel	God is my judge	Hebrew
Danny	God has judged	Scottish

Dante	enduring	Latin
Darian	gift	Greek
Dariel	open	French
Dario	wealthy	Greek
Darius	preserver	Persian
Darrell	open	French
Darren	great	Gaelic
Darwin	dear friend	English
Dash	from Chiel	English
Davian	beloved	American
David	beloved	Hebrew
Davin	dearly loved	Hebrew
Davion	beloved	English
Davis	David's son	English
Dawson	David's son	English
Dax	a town in south-western France	French
Daxton	reference to the French town Dax	English
Dayton	day town	English
Deacon	dusty one	English
Dean	church official	English
Deandre	combination of prefix De and Andre	American
Deangelo	from the angel	Italian
Declan	man of prayer	Irish
Demetrius	of Demeter	Latin
Dennis	from Dionysius (mythical God of wine)	English
Denver	from Anvers	English, French
Derek	the peoples ruler	English
Derrick	gifted ruler	English

Deshawn	God is gracious	African American
Desmond	from South Munster	Gaelic
Devin	poet	Irish
Devon	poet	Irish
Dexter	right handed	Latin
Diego	supplanter	Spanish
Dilan	like a lion	Irish
Dillon	like a lion	Irish
Dimitri	earth-lover	Greek
Dominic	belonging to the lord	Latin
Dominick	of the Lord	Latin
Dominik	belonging to the lord	Slavic, German
Dominique	of the lord	French
Donald	great chief	Scottish
Donovan	brown-haired chieftain	Irish
Dorian	of Doris, a district of Greece	Greek
Douglas	dark water	Scottish
Drake	dragon	Greek
Draven	of the raven	American
Drew	manly	Scottish
Duke	English rank of nobility	English
Duncan	dark warrior	Scottish
Dustin	a fighter	English
Dwayne	dark	Irish
Dylan	son of the wave	Welsh
Ean	the Lord is gracious	Scottish
Easton	from East town	English
Eddie	rich in friendship	English
Eden	delight	Hebrew
Edgar	fortunate and powerful	English
Edison	son of Edward	English
Eduardo	wealthy guardian	English

Edward	wealthy guardian	English
Edwin	wealthy friend	English
Eli	my God	Hebrew
Elian	the Lord is my God	Hebrew, Welsh
Elias	Yaweh is God	Hebrew
Elijah	Yaweh is God	Hebrew
Eliseo	God is salvation	Italian, Spanish
Elisha	God is salvation	Hebrew
Elliot	Jehovah is God	Greek
Elliott	Jehovah is God	Greek
Ellis	Jehovah is God	Greek
Emanuel	God with us	Hebrew
Emerson	brave; powerful	German
Emery	brave; powerful	German
Emiliano	work	Italian, Spanish
Emilio	industrious	Latin
Emmanuel	God is with us	Hebrew
Emmet	universal	English, German
Emmett	universal	English, German
Emmitt	universal	English, German
Emory	brave	English
Enoch	dedicated	Hebrew
Enrique	rules his household	Spanish
Enzo	winner	Italian
Ephraim	fruitful; productive	Hebrew
Eric	eternal ruler	Norse
Erick	ruler of the people	Norse
Erik	ever kingly	Scandinavian
Ernest	serious and determined	German
Ernesto	serious and determined	Spanish
Esteban	crowned in victory	Spanish
Ethan	strong	Hebrew
Eugene	wellborn	Greek

Evan	young	Welsh
Everett	brave as a wild boar	English
Ezekiel	God strengthens	Hebrew
Ezequiel	God strengthens	Spanish, Portuguese
Ezra	help	Hebrew
Fabian	bean grower	Latin
Felipe	friend of horses	Spanish
Felix	happy	Latin
Fernando	adventurer	Spanish
Finley	fair-haired hero	Irish, Scottish
Finn	fair	Irish
Finnegan	fair	Irish
Finnley	fair warrior	Irish
Fisher	fisherman	English
Fletcher	arrow maker	English
Flynn	son of the red-haired one	Irish
Ford	dweller at the ford	English
Forrest	dweller near the woods	English
Francis	Frenchman or free man	Latin
Francisco	Frenchman or free man	Spanish
Franco	Frenchman or free man	Spanish
Frank	Frenchman or free man	French
Frankie	Frenchman or free man	French
Franklin	free born landowner	English
Freddy	peaceful ruler	German
Frederick	peaceful ruler	German
Gabriel	man of God	Hebrew
Gael	stranger	Irish, American
Gage	oath; pledge	French
Gannon	fair-skinned and fair-haired	Irish
Garrett	spear strength	Irish

Gary	hard or bold spear	English
Gauge	pledge	French
Gavin	white hawk	Celtic
George	farmer	Greek
Gerald	ruler with the spear	English
Gerardo	spear courageous	Spanish
Giancarlo	God's gracious gift	Italian
Gianni	God is gracious	Italian
Gibson	Gilbert's son	English
Gideon	hewer; having a stump for a hand	Hebrew
Gilbert	shining pledge	German
Giovani	God is gracious	Italian
Giovanni	God is gracious	Italian
Gordon	great hill	Scottish
Grady	noble and illustrious	Irish
Graham	gravelly homestead	Scottish
Grant	large	Scottish
Graysen	the son of the bailiff	English
Grayson	the son of the bailiff	English
Gregory	vigilant; a watchman	Greek
Grey	gray-haired	English
Greyson	son of Gregory	American
Griffin	strong lord	Welsh
Guillermo	resolute protector	Spanish
Gunnar	bold warrior	Scandinavian
Gunner	battle strong	Swedish
Gustavo	royal staff	Spanish
Haiden	fire	English
Hamza	sour leaves	Muslim
Hank	estate ruler	German
Harlan	from the hare's land	English
Harley	hare clearing	English

Harold	army ruler	Scandinavian
Harper	harpist; minstrel	English
Harrison	son of Harry	English
Harry	estate ruler	English
Harvey	battle worthy	French
Hassan	handsome	Muslim
Hayden	from the hedged in valley	English
Hayes	hedged area	English
Heath	untended land where flowering shrubs grow	English
Hector	holding fast	Greek
Hendrix	estate ruler	Dutch, German
Henrik	estate ruler	Danish, Hungarian
Henry	estate ruler	German
Hezekiah	God is my strength	Hebrew
Holden	from the hollow in the valley	English
Houston	from Hugh's town	Scottish
Hudson	Hugh's son	English
Hugh	intellect	English
Hugo	intellect	Latin
Hunter	one who hunts	English
Huxley	inhospitable place	English
Ian	the Lord is gracious	Scottish
Ibrahim	a prophet's name	Muslim
Ignacio	fiery	Spanish
Iker	visitation	Basque
Immanuel	God is with us	Hebrew
Isaac	laughter	Hebrew
Isaiah	salvation of the Lord	Hebrew
Isaias	God's helper	Hebrew

Ishaan	the sun	Hindi
Ismael	God listens	Hebrew
Israel	may God prevail	Hebrew
Issac	laughter	Hebrew
Ivan	gracious gift from God	Russian
Izaiah	God is salvation	Hebrew
Jabari	brave	Egyptian
Jace	a healing	Greek
Jack	God is gracious	English
Jackson	God is gracious	Scottish
Jacob	supplanter	Hebrew
Jacoby	supplanter	Hebrew
Jaden	Jehovah has heard	Hebrew
Jadiel	God has heard	Spanish
Jadon	thankful	Hebrew
Jagger	carter	English
Jaiden	God has heard	Hebrew
Jaime	supplanter	Spanish
Jairo	Jehovah enlightens	Spanish
Jake	he grasps the heel	Hebrew
Jakob	supplanter	Hebrew
Jalen	from James and Lenore	American
Jamal	handsome	Arabic
Jamari	handsome	American
Jamarion	grace	American
James	supplanter	English
Jameson	son of James	English
Jamie	supplanter	Hebrew
Jamir	handsome	Arabic
Jamison	supplanter	English
Jared	descending	Hebrew
Jase	a healing	Greek
Jasiah	God supports	Hebrew

Jason	a healing	Greek
Jasper	bringer of treasure	Persian
Javier	bright	Spanish
Javion	elaboration of Javon	American
Javon	"Greece"	Hebrew
Jax	God has been gracious	English
Jaxen	son of Jack	English
Jaxon	Gid has been gracious	English
Jaxson	son of Jack	English
Jaxton	a product of American imagination	American
Jay	to rejoice	English
Jayce	a healing	Greek
Jayceon	one who makes people feel better	Greek
Jayden	thankful	Hebrew
Jaydon	Jehovah has heard	Hebrew
Jaylen	jaybird	American
Jayson	a healing	Greek
Jayvion	offers advice	Hebrew
Jaziel	chosen by God	Hebrew
Jedidiah	beloved of the Lord	Hebrew
Jefferson	son of Geoffrey	English
Jeffery	traveller	German
Jeffrey	traveller	German
Jensen	son of Jens	English
Jeremiah	may Jehovah exalt	Hebrew
Jeremy	may Jehovah exalt	Hebrew
Jermaine	brotherly	Latin
Jerome	holy name	Greek
Jerry	may Jehovah exalt	Hebrew
Jesse	wealthy	Hebrew
Jessie	wealthy	Hebrew

Jesus	Jehovah is salvation	Latin
Jett	free	American
Jimmy	supplanter	Hebrew
Joaquin	God will judge	Spanish
Joe	may Jehovah add	Hebrew
Joel	Jehovah is his God	Hebrew
Joey	may Jehovah add	Hebrew
Johan	God is gracious	German
John	Jehovah has been gracious	Hebrew
Johnathan	Jehovah has give	Hebrew
Johnny	Jehovah's gift	Hebrew
Jon	Jehovah has been gracious	English
Jonael	honest	Hispanic
Jonah	dove	Hebrew
Jonas	gift from God	Hebrew
Jonathan	Jehovah has given	Hebrew
Jonathon	gift of Jehovah	Hebrew
Jordan	to flow down	Hebrew
Jordy	down flowing	Hebrew
Jordyn	flowing down	Hebrew
Jorge	farmer	Spanish
Jose	may God give increase	Spanish
Joseph	may Jehovah add	Hebrew
Joshua	Jehovah is generous	Hebrew
Josiah	Jehovah has healed	Hebrew
Josue	God is salvation	Hebrew
Jovani	form of Jovan 'Father of the sky'	Latin
Joziah	Jehovah has healed	Hebrew
Juan	God is gracious	Spanish

Judah	praised	Hebrew
Jude	praised	Latin
Judson	descend	Hebrew
Juelz	modern invented name	American
Julian	youthful	Latin
Julien	youthful	French
Julio	youthful	Latin
Julius	downy-bearded	Latin
Junior	younger	Latin
Justice	righteous	Latin
Justin	just	Latin
Justus	upright	Biblical
Kade	from the wetlands	Gaelic
Kaden	companion	Arabic
Kaeden	fighter	Gaelic
Kai	sea	Hawaiian
Kaiden	battler	American
Kaison	rebel	American
Kaleb	brave	Hebrew
Kalel	friend	Arabic
Kamari	moonlight	African
Kamden	winding valley	Scottish
Kamdyn	winding valley	Scottish
Kameron	crooked nose	Scottish
Kamren	modern variant of Cameron for girls	English
Kamron	crooked nose	Scottish
Kamryn	modern variant of Cameron for girls	English
Kane	warrior	Celtic
Kannon	form of Kuan-yin who was Chinese Buddhist	Japanese

Kareem	generous	Arabic
Karson	a follower of Christ	English
Karter	transporter of goods by cart	English
Kase	belonging to Case	French
Kasen	helmeted	Latin
Kash	hollow	American
Kashton	makes friends easily	American
Kason	house	American
Kayden	son of Cadan	Irish
Kaysen	a contemporary name	American
Kayson	healer	American
Keagan	a thinker	Irish
Keaton	place of hawks	English
Keegan	a thinker	Irish
Keenan	ancient	Irish
Keith	dwells in the woods	Welsh
Kellan	slender	German, Irish
Kellen	slender	German, Irish
Kelvin	river man	English
Kendall	royal valley	English
Kendrick	greatest champion	Welsh
Kenneth	handsome	Scottish
Kenny	handsome	Irish
Kevin	handsome by birth	Irish
Khalil	companion	Arabic
Kian	ancient	Irish
Kieran	dark skinned	Gaelic
Killian	war strife or church	Irish
King	king	English
Kingsley	from the king's meadow	English
Kingston	from the king's village	English
Knox	from the hills	English

Kobe	tortoise	Swahili
Kody	helpful	English
Kohen	priest	Hebrew
Kolby	dark-haired	German
Kole	swarthy	English
Kolten	coal town	German
Kolton	coal town	German
Konnor	lover of hounds	Irish
Korbin	crow	Latin
Kristian	follower of Christ	English
Kristopher	form of Christopher	Scandinavian
Kye	rejoice	Latin
Kylan	a place name referring to the narrows	Gaelic
Kyle	a place name referring to the narrows	Gaelic
Kylen	a place name referring to the narrows	Gaelic
Kyler	a place name referring to the narrows	Gaelic
Kymani	adventurous traveller	Eastern African
Kyree	Lord	Greek
Kyrie	Lord	Greek
Kyson	son of Kyle	English
Lachlan	warlike	Scottish
Lamar	of the sea	French
Lance	land	French
Landen	long hill	English
Landon	long hill	English
Landry	ruler	French, English
Landyn	long hill	English

Lane	from the long meadow path	English
Langston	from the long enclosure	English
Larry	of Laurentum	Latin
Lawrence	of Laurentum	Latin
Lawson	son of Lawrence	English
Layne	roadway	English
Layton	settlement with a leek garden	Old English
Leandro	lion-made	Spanish, Portuguese, Italian
Lee	meadow or wood	English
Legend	story	English, Latin
Leighton	herb garden	English
Leland	from the meadow land	English
Lennon	lover	Irish
Lennox	with many elm trees	Scottish
Leo	lion	Latin
Leon	lion	French
Leonard	brave lion	German
Leonardo	lion-bold	Portuguese
Leonel	young lion	Spanish
Leonidas	lion	Latin
Leroy	the king	French
Levi	attached	Hebrew
Lewis	renowned warrior	English
Liam	resolute protection	Irish
Lincoln	Roman colony at the pool	English
Lionel	young lion	French
Lochlan	from the fjord-land	Scottish
Logan	small hollow	Scottish

London	fortress of the moon	Latin
Lorenzo	from the place of laurel trees	Spanish
Louie	famous warrior	French
Louis	famous warrior	French
Luca	man from Lucania	Italian
Lucas	man from Lucania	Latin
Lucca	man from Lucania	Italian
Lucian	form of Luke; illumination	American
Luciano	form of Luke; illumination	American
Luis	famous fighter	German
Luka	light	Latin
Lukas	light	Latin
Luke	light giving	Greek
Lyric	of the lyre	French
Mack	son of	Celtic
Madden	little dog	Irish
Maddox	son of Maddock	Welsh
Magnus	greatest	Latin
Maison	house	French
Major	greater	Latin
Makai	toward the sea	Hawiian
Malachi	my messenger	Hebrew
Malakai	my messenger	Hebrew
Malaki	my messenger	Hebrew
Malcolm	devotee of St. Colombia	Scottish
Malik	master	Arabic
Manuel	God is with us	Hebrew
Marc	derived from Latin Marcus	English

Marcel	form of the Latin Marcellus	French
Marcelo	hammer	Italian
Marco	Mars (Roman God of war)	Italian
Marcos	of Mars	Portuguese
Marcus	hammer	Latin
Mario	hammer	Latin
Mark	warlike	Latin
Markus	of Mars	German
Marley	pleasant seaside meadow	English
Marlon	little falcon	French
Marquis	title name ranking below duke and above earl	French
Marshall	love of horses	Scottish
Martin	of Mars	Latin
Marvin	from the sea fortress	Welsh
Mason	worker in stone	English
Mateo	God's gift	Spanish
Mathew	gift of God	Hebrew
Mathias	gift of God	Aramaic
Matias	gift of God	Spanish, Finnish
Matteo	gift of God	Hebrew, Italian
Matthew	gift of God	Hebrew
Matthias	gift from God	Hebrew
Maurice	dark-skinned	Latin
Mauricio	dark-skinned	Spanish
Maverick	independent	American
Max	greatest	English, German
Maxim	the greatest	Latin
Maximilian	greatest	Latin
Maximiliano	the greatest	Italian
Maximo	the greatest	Italian
Maximus	greatest	Latin

38

Maxton	greatest	English
Maxwell	Magnus' spring	Scottish
Mayson	worker in stone	English
Mekhi	who is like God	Hebrew
Melvin	chief	Irish
Memphis	enduring and beautiful	Greek, Coptic
Messiah	anointed one	Hebrew
Micah	who is like the Lord	Hebrew
Michael	gift from God	Hebrew
Micheal	who is like God	Gaelic
Miguel	who is like God	Portuguese
Milan	gracious	Stavic
Miles	soldier or merciful	English
Miller	grinder of grain	English
Milo	soldier	Latin, Old German
Misael	as God is	Hebrew
Mitchell	gift from God	Hebrew
Mohamed	glorified	Arabic
Mohammad	praiseworthy	Arabic
Mohammed	glorified	Arabic
Moises	from the water	Spanish
Morgan	bright sea	Welsh
Moses	delivered from the water	Egyptian
Moshe	delivered from the water	Hebrew
Muhammad	praiseworthy	Arabic
Musa	a prophet's name	Muslim
Mustafa	chosen	Muslim
Myles	destroyer	Greek
Nash	by the ash tree	English
Nasir	supporter	Muslim
Nathan	gift from God	Hebrew
Nathanael	gift of God	Biblical
Nathaniel	gift of God	Biblical

Nehemiah	comforted by God	Hebrew
Neil	champion	Gaelic
Nelson	son of the champion	Irish
Neymar	unknown meaning	Brazilian
Nicholas	people of victory	Greek
Nickolas	victorious	Slavic
Nico	victorious	English
Nicolas	people's victory	Greek
Niko	victorious	English
Nikolai	victory of the people	East Slavic
Nikolas	victorious	Slavic
Nixon	victorious	English
Noah	comfort	Hebrew
Noe	consolation	Biblical
Noel	Christmas	French
Nolan	champion	Irish
Oakley	from the oak tree	English
Odin	wealthy	Anglo-Saxon
Oliver	the olive tree	English
Omar	eloquent	Hebrew
Omari	God the highest	African
Orion	rising in the sky	Greek
Orlando	famous land	Spanish
Oscar	divine spear	English
Osvaldo	divine power	Teutonic
Otis	wealthy	German
Otto	born eighth or wealthy	German
Owen	young warrior	Welsh
Pablo	small	Spanish
Parker	keeper of the forest	English
Patrick	noble	English
Paul	small	Latin
Paxton	from the peaceful farm	English

Payton	noble	Irish
Pedro	the merchant of Venice	American
Peter	a rock	English
Peyton	royal	Scottish
Philip	lover of horses	Greek
Phillip	lover of horses	Greek
Phoenix	bird reborn from its own ashes	Greek
Pierce	form of Piers from Peter	Irish
Porter	gatekeeper	French
Preston	priest's town	English
Prince	principal one	English
Princeton	principal one	Latin
Quentin	born fifth	Latin
Quincy	born fifth	Latin
Quinn	counsel	Gaelic
Quintin	fifth	Latin
Quinton	born fifth	Latin
Rafael	God has healed	Hebrew
Raiden	thunder and lightning	Japanese
Ramon	form of Raymond 'Guards wisely	Spanish
Randy	house wolf	English
Raphael	God has healed	Hebrew
Rashad	thinker	Arabic
Raul	form of Ralph 'wolf counsel'	Spanish
Ray	guards wisely	German
Rayan	land lush and rich in water	Arabic
Rayden	no meaning	American

Raylan	modern twist on Raymond	American
Raymond	wise protector	Teutonic
Reagan	regal	Celtic
Reece	ardent	English
Reed	redheaded	English
Reese	fiery	Welsh
Reginald	powerful ruler	German
Reid	redheaded	Scottish
Remington	from the raven farm	English
Remy	rower	French
Rene	reborn	French
Reuben	the vision of the son	Biblical
Rex	king	Latin
Rey	king	Spanish
Reyansh	ray of light	Hindi
Rhett	fiery	Welsh
Rhys	ardour; rashness	Welsh
Riaan	little king	Hindi
Ricardo	strong ruler	Spanish
Richard	powerful; strong ruler	German
Ricky	gifted ruler	English
Ridge	from the ridge	English
Riley	valiant	Gaelic
River	riverbank	Old French
Robert	bright; shining	German
Roberto	bright; shining	Portuguese
Robin	bright; shining	German
Rocco	rock	Italian
Rocky	rock	English
Rodney	island of reeds	English
Rodolfo	famous wolf	Spanish
Rodrigo	famous ruler	Portuguese

Rogelio	famous soldier	Spanish
Roger	farmed spear	English
Rohan	ascending	Sanskrit
Roland	renowned in the land	English
Rolando	renowned in the land	French
Roman	man of Rome	Latin
Romeo	a pilgrim to Rome	Italian
Ronald	mighty counsellor	Scottish
Ronan	oath	Celtic
Ronin	little seal	Irish
Ronnie	mighty counsellor	Scottish
Rory	red	Irish
Rowan	red	Gaelic
Rowen	red haired	Irish
Roy	red haired	Celtic
Royal	red	Gaelic
Royce	royal	English
Ruben	behold a son	Hebrew
Rudy	famed wolf	German
Russell	red haired	Latin
Ryan	kingly	Irish
Ryder	knight	American
Ryker	hardy power	Danish
Rylan	island meadow	Irish
Ryland	from the rye land	English
Sage	wise one	English
Salvador	savior	Spanish
Salvatore	savior	Italian
Sam	sun child	Hebrew
Samir	jovial	Muslim
Samson	bright sun	Hebrew
Samuel	heard by God	Hebrew
Santana	place name	Spanish

Santiago	named for Saint James	Spanish
Santino	little saint	Italian
Santos	saint	Spanish
Saul	inquired for God	Hebrew
Sawyer	cuts timber	Celtic
Scott	from Scotland	English
Seamus	form of James; supplanter	Gaelic
Sean	gift from God	Irish
Sebastian	venerable	Latin
Sergio	attendant	Italian
Seth	anointed	Hebrew
Shane	God is gracious	Irish
Shaun	God is gracious	Irish
Shawn	gift from God	Irish
Shiloh	the one to whom it belongs	Hebrew
Silas	of the forest	Latin
Simon	snubnosed	Greek
Sincere	earnest	American
Skylar	phonetic spelling of Schuyler	English
Skyler	phonetic spelling of Schuyler	English
Solomon	peace	Hebrew
Sonny	son	American
Soren	strict	Scandinavian
Spencer	keeper of provisions	American
Stanley	stone leigh	Old English
Stefan	crowned with laurels'	Russian
Stephen	crown	Greek
Sterling	pure	English

Stetson	nickname for a boxer	Anglo-Saxon
Steve	victorious	Greek
Steven	crown	English
Sullivan	dark eyes	American
Sutton	from the south farm	English
Sylas	wood or forest	English
Talon	claw	English
Tanner	worker in leather	English
Tate	he who talks too much	Native American
Tatum	brings joy	English
Taylor	tailor	English
Terrance	Roman clan name	Latin
Terrell	thunder ruler	English
Terrence	smooth	Latin
Terry	powerful	Germanic
Thaddeus	praise	Aramaic
Thatcher	roofer	English
Theo	God given	Greek
Theodore	God-given	Greek
Thiago	supplanter	Spanish
Thomas	twin	Aramaic
Timothy	God's honour	Greek
Titan	defender	Greek
Titus	pleasing	Biblical
Tobias	from the Hebrew Tobiah	Spanish
Toby	abbreviation of Tobias	English
Todd	fox	English
Tomas	twin	Gaelic
Tommy	twin	Aramaic
Tony	highly praiseworthy	English
Trace	brave	Anglo-Saxon
Travis	crossroads	English

Trent	refers to English river Trent	English
Trenton	refers to the English river Trent	English
Trevor	prudent	Irish
Trey	three	English
Tripp	traveler	English
Tristan	outcry	French
Tristen	outcry	Arthurian
Triston	outcry	French
Troy	derives from ancient Greek city of Troy	English
Truman	loyal	English
Tucker	Tucker of doth	English
Turner	lathe worker	English
Ty	earth	English Irish
Tyler	tile layer	English
Tyrone	from Owen's territory	Irish
Tyson	son of a German	French
Ulises	Greek name Odysseus	Spanish
Uriah	God is my light	Hebrew
Uriel	God is my light	Hebrew
Urijah	the Lord is my light or fire	Biblical
Wade	river crossing	English
Valentin	strong	Spanish
Valentino	brave or strong	Italian
Walker	worker in cloth	English
Walter	powerful ruler	German
Van	equivalent of 'de' in French names	Dutch
Vance	marshland	English

Warren	protector	German
Vaughn	little	Welsh
Waylon	land beside the road	English
Wayne	craftsman	English
Wesley	from the west meadow	English
Westin	west town	English
Weston	west town	English
Vicente	conquering	Portuguese
Victor	conqueror	Latin
Vihaan	dawn	Sanskrit
Wilder	wild	American
Will	will-helmet	German
William	resolute protector	German
Willie	will-helmet	German
Wilson	son of Will	English
Vincent	conquering	Latin
Vincenzo	conqueror	Latin
Winston	from a friend's town	English
Vivaan	full of life	Hindi
Wyatt	guide	English
Xander	defending men	Greek
Xavier	new house or bright	Basque, Arabic
Xzavier	new house or bright	Arabic
Yadiel	God has heard	Spanish
Yahir	he will enlighten	Hebrew, Arabic
Yahya	a prophet's name	Muslim
Yehuda	praised	Hebrew
Yosef	God shall add	Hebrew
Yousef	God increases	Arabic
Yusuf	God increases	Arabic
Zachariah	Jehovah has remembered	Hebrew
Zachary	Remembered by God	Hebrew
Zackary	God has remembered	Hebrew

Zaid	he shall add	Egyptian
Zaiden	lucky one	Hebrew
Zain	beauty	Muslim
Zaire	the river that swallows all rivers	African-American
Zander	to defend	Latin
Zane	gift from God	Hebrew
Zavier	new house	Basque Spanish
Zayden	little fire	Celtic American
Zayn	grace	Arabic
Zayne	grace	Arabic
Zechariah	Jehovah has remembered	Hebrew
Zeke	God strengthens	Hebrew
Zion	monument	Biblical

Girls Names

Name	Meaning	origin
Aaliyah	highborn	Arabic
Abby	father's joy	Hebrew
Abigail	my father is joyful	Hebrew
Abril	symbolizes spring	Spanish
Ada	nobility	French
Adaline	noble	Teutonic
Adalyn	noble	French
Adalynn	noble	French
Addilyn	noble	French
Addilynn	noble	French
Addison	son of Adam	Old English
Addisyn	son of Adam	American, Scottish
Addyson	form of Addison; son of Adam	English
Adelaide	nobility	French
Adele	kind and tender	Germanic
Adelina	noble	Italian, Spanish, Portuguese
Adeline	pleasant	German
Adelyn	nobility	German
Adelynn	nobility	German
Adilynn	nobility	German
Adley	judicious	Hebrew
Adriana dark	Latin	
Adrianna	dark	French
Adrienne	the dark one	French
Aileen	light	Irish

49

Aimee	dearly loved	French
Ainsley	one's own meadow	Scottish
Aisha	life	Muslim
Aislinn	dream	Irish
Aitana	the glorious one	Portuguese
Aiyana	eternal blossom	Native American
Alaia	joyful	Basque
Alaina	harmony	Irish
Alana	little rock	Irish
Alani	dear child	Irish
Alanna	child	Gaelic
Alannah	little rock	Irish
Alaya	dwelling	Sanskrit
Alayah	heavens	Arabic
Alayna	dear child	Irish
Aleah	God's being	Arabic, Persian
Aleena	good-looking	Celtic
Alejandra	defender of mankind	Spanish
Alena	light	Greek
Alessandra	defender of men	Greek
Alexa	defending men	Greek
Alexandra	defending men	Greek
Alexandria	defending men	Greek
Alexia	helper	Greek
Alexis	defender	Greek
Alia	supreme	Arabic
Aliana	my God has answered	Hebrew
Alianna	my God has answered	Hebrew
Alice	nobility	French
Alicia	nobility	Latin
Alina	noble	German
Alisha	protected by God	Sanskrit
Alison	noble	Norman French

Alissa	noble humor	Teutonic
Alisson	noble	French
Alivia	olive tree	Latin
Aliya	heavens	Arabic
Aliyah	highest social standing	Muslim
Aliza	joy	Hebrew
Allie	harmony	Celtic
Allison	noble	Scottish
Ally	harmony	Celtic
Allyson	noble	Scottish
Alma	kind	Latin
Alondra	defender of mankind	Spanish
Alyson	honest	Irish
Alyssa	rational	Greek
Amalia	hard working	Italian
Amanda	lovable	Latin
Amani	wishes	American
Amara	grace or bitter	Igbo, Latin
Amari	eternal	Hebrew
Amaris	given by God	Hebrew
Amaya	night rain	Spanish
Amber	powerful and complete	American
Amelia	work	German
Amelie	hard working	French
America	land of the prince	Latin
Amia	beloved	French
Amina	trustworthy	Muslim
Aminah	trustworthy	Arabic
Amira	princess; one who speaks	Hebrew
Amirah	princess; one who speaks	Hebrew
Amiya	delight	Indian

Amiyah	delight	Indian
Amy	dearly loved	French
Amya	no meaning	American
Ana	grace	Spanish
Anabella	beautiful; graceful	Latin
Anabelle	loving	French
Anahi	the immaculate	Spanish
Analia	combination of Ana and Lucia	Spanish
Anastasia	resurrection	Greek
Anaya	answer of God	Hebrew
Andi	brave	English
Andrea	manly	Greek
Angel	messenger or angel	Greek
Angela	messenger or agel	Greek
Angelica	like an angel	Latin
Angelina	messenger or angel	Greek
Angeline	messenger or angel	Greek
Angelique	like and angel	French
Angie	messenger or angel	Greek
Anika	sweetness or face	Nordic
Aniya	God has shown meaning	Polish
Aniyah	ship	Hebrew
Ann	merciful	English
Anna	grace	Hebrew
Annabel	loving	Scottish
Annabella	beautful; graceful	Latin
Annabelle	loving	Scottish
Annalee	biblical	Latin
Annalise	graced with God's bounty	Latin

Anne	favour or grace	Hebrew
Annie	frequently used as an independent name	English
Annika	gracious	Swedish
Ansley	clearing with a hermitage	English
Anya	grace	Russian
April	symbolizes spring	Latin
Arabella	derived from 'orabilis' meaning yeilding to prayer	Latin
Aranzaamong	the thorns	Basque
Arden	valley of the eagle	English
Arely	lion of God	American, Hebrew, Spanish
Aria	lioness	Italian, Hebrew
Ariadne	most holy	Greek
Ariah	most holy	Greek
Ariana	holy	Latin
Arianna	holy	Latin
Ariel	sprite; lion of God	Hebrew
Ariella	lion of God	Hebrew
Arielle	lion of God	Hebrew
Ariya	lioness	Hebrew
Ariyah	lioness	Hebrew
Armani	castle	Hebrew
Arya	noble goddess	Indian
Aryana	most holy	Italian
Aryanna	most holy	Italian
Ashley	lives in the ash tree grove	English
Ashlyn	dream	Irish

Ashlynn	dream	Irish
Asia	muddy; boggy	Biblical
Aspen	aspen tree	American, English
Astrid	godly strength	Scandinavian
Athena	goddess of wisdom	Greek
Aubree	rules with elf-wisdom	French
Aubrey	blond ruler; elf ruler	French
Aubrianna	combination of Aubrey and Anna	American
Aubrie	rules with elf-wisdom	English
Aubriella	combination of Aubrey and Ella	American
Aubrielle	elf ruler	American
Audrey	noble strength	English
Audrina	noble strength	English
Aurelia	the golden one	Latin
Aurora	Roman goddess of the dawn	Latin
Autumn	born in the fall	English
Ava	life	Latin
Avah	life	Latin
Avalyn	beautiful breath of life	Old English
Avalynn	beautiful breath of life	Old English
Averi	ruler of the elves	English
Averie	ruler of the elves	English
Avery	ruler of the elves	English
Aviana	bird	Latin
Avianna	bird	Latin
Aya	to fly swiftly	Hebrew
Ayla	oak tree	Hebrew
Ayleen	bright shining light	Irish
Aylin	moon halo	Turkish

Azalea	dry	Greek
Azaria	helped by God	Hebrew
Azariah	helped by God	Hebrew
Bailee	steward; bailiff	English
Bailey	public official	English
Barbara	from the Greek barbarous meaning foreign or strange	English
Baylee	steward; bailiff	English
Beatrice	she who brings happiness	Latin
Belen	arrow	Greek
Bella	beautiful; lovable; graceful	Latin
Bethany	the house of song	Biblical
Bianca	white; shining	Italian
Blair	from the fields	Irish
Blake	kight; dark	English
Blakely	from the light meadow; from dark meadow	English
Bonnie	pretty; charming	Scottish
Braelyn	primrose	American
Braelynn	primrose	American
Braylee	no meaning	American
Breanna	strong and virtuous	American
Brenda	sword or torch	Scottish
Brenna	beacon on the hill Little raven	Irish
Bria	hill	Irish
Briana	strong and virtuous	American
Brianna	strong and virtuous	American

Briar	a thorny patch	English
Bridget	the high one oe strength	Irish
Briella	God is my strength	Hebrew
Brielle	hunting grounds	French
Briley	woodland	American
Brinley	burnt wood	English
Bristol	a place name	English
Brittany	originally the ancient duchy of Bretagne in France	English
Brooke	lives by the stream	English
Brooklyn	water	English
Brooklynn	water	English
Bryanna	strong	Celtic
Brylee	combination of Bryan and Lee	American
Bryleigh	combination of Bryan and Leigh	American
Brynlee	hill; mound	Welsh
Brynn	hill	Welsh
Cadence	a rhythmic flow of sounds	English
Caitlin	pure; clear	French
Caitlyn	meaning pure	Irish
Cali	most beautiful	Greek
Callie	most beautiful	Greek
Cameron	crooked nose	Scottish
Camila	free-born	Latin
Camilla	servant for the temple	Latin
Camille	French form of Camilla or Camillus	French

Camryn	crooked nose	Scottish
Cara	beloved	Italian
Carla	Germanic form of Charles meaning a man	German
Carlee	free man	American
Carly	free man	American
Carmen	garden	Spanish
Carolina	strong	Latin
Caroline	strong	Italian
Carolyn	strong	Italian
Carter	transporter of goods by cart	English
Casey	from a polish word meaning 'proclamation of peace'	English
Cassandra	unheeded prophetess	Greek
Cassidy	intelligent	Irish
Cataleya	flower name	English
Catalina	from the Greek Catherine meaning pure	Portuguese
Catherine	pure	French
Caylee	slender	Gaelic
Cecelia	blind	Latin
Cecilia	blind	Latin
Celeste	based on the Latin caelestis meaning heavenly	French
Celia	heavenly	Latin
Celine	Latin 'caelum' meaning sky or heaven	French

Chana	graceful	Hebrew
Chanel	canal; channel	French
Charlee	manly	English
Charleigh	free man	English
Charley	from Old English 'ceorl' meaning man	English
Charli	manly	English
Charlie	manly	English
Charlize	free man	English
Charlotte	free man	French
Chaya	life	Hebrew
Chelsea	seaport	English
Cherish	to treasure and care for	English, Old French
Cheyenne	an Algonquian tribe of the Great Plains	French
Chloe	green shoot; fresh blooming	Greek
Christina	follower of Christ	Latin
Christine	follower of Christ	French
Ciara	saint of dark	American
Claire	bright; clear	French
Clara	bright or clear	Latin
Clare	illustrious	Latin
Clarissa	gentle; famous	English
Claudia	lame	French
Clementine, from 'Clemens'	meaning mild or peaceful	Latin
Colette	necklace	French
Collins	abbreviation of Nicolas meaning people's victory	English

Cora	girl or maiden	Greek
Coraline	from the coral of the sea	Greek
Cordelia	daughter of the sea	Latin, Celtic
Corinne	maiden	French
Courtney	from the court or short nose	French
Crystal	gem name	Scottish
Cynthia	of Cynthus	Greek
Dahlia	from the valley	Norse
Daisy	Day's eye	English
Dakota	friend; ally	Native American
Dalary	modern invented name	American
Daleyza	delightful	Spanish
Dallas	from the waterfall	Gaelic
Dana	from Denmark	English
Danica	morning star	Slavic
Daniela	God is my judge	Hebrew
Daniella	God has judged	Hebrew
Danielle	God is my judge	French
Danna	feminine God will judge	English
Daphne	bay tree or laurel tree	Greek
Dayana	divine	Latin
Deborah	bee	Hebrew
Delaney	competitor's child; from the river Slaney	Irish
Delilah	amorous; temptress	Hebrew
Demi	abbreviation of Demetria-mythological goddess of harvest	English

Denise	feminine form of Dennis	French
Desiree	desired	French
Destiny	certain fortune; fate	English
Diana	fertile	Latin
Dixie	refers to French word for ten	English
Dorothy	gift of God	English
Dulce	sweet	Latin
Dylan	born near the sea	Welsh
Eden	delight	Hebrew
Edith	happy warfare	English
Eileen	from a surname meaning hazelnut	French
Elaina	shining light	French
Elaine	bright shining light	Old French
Eleanor	shining light	American
Elena	bright one	Spanish
Eliana	Jehovah is God	Hebrew
Elianna	God has answered me	Latin
Elin	most beautiful woman	Welsh
Elisa	consecrated to God	Spanish
Elisabeth	oath of God; God is satisfaction	Hebrew
Elise	oath of God	Greek
Eliza	oath of God	Greek
Elizabeth	God is satisfaction	Greek
Ella	beautiful fairy	English
Elle	beautiful fairy	English
Ellen	courage	Anglo-Saxon
Elliana	my God has answered	Latin
Ellie	most beautiful woman	English

Elliot	Jehovah is God	Greek
Elliott	Jehovah is God	Greek
Ellis	Jehovah is God	Greek
Ellison	son of elder	English
Eloise	famous in war	French
Elora	the crown of victory	English
Elsa	oath of God	Greek
Elsie	my God is bountiful; God is plenty	Scottish
Elyse	from the blessed isles	Greek
Ember	hot ashes	English
Emelia	industrious; striving	Latin
Emely	rival	Latin
Emerie	industrious	German
Emerson	Emery's son; brave	German
Emersyn	son of Emery	English
Emery	industrious	German
Emilee	striving	Latin
Emilia	industrious	Italian
Emilie	striving	Latin
Emily	industrious	Latin
Emma	whole	German
Emmalee	industrious	Latin
Emmaline	hardworking	French
Emmalyn	combination of Emma and Lyn	English
Emmalynn	combination of Emma and Lynn	English
Emmeline	industrious	French
Emmy	hardworking	German
Emory	brave; powerful	English
Erica	ever kingly	Scandinavian

Erika	eternal ruler	Norse
Erin	peace; poetic name for Ireland	Gaelic
Esme	esteemed; emerald	French, Persian
Esmeralda	the emerald gemstone	Spanish
Esperanza	hope	Spanish
Estella	star	French
Estelle	star	Latin
Esther	refers to the planet Venus; star	Persian
Estrella	star	Spanish
Eva	living one	Latin
Evalyn	form of Evelyn; life	English
Evangeline	bringer of good news	Greek
Eve	lively	Hebrew
Evelyn	hazelnut	French
Evelynn	hazelnut	French
Everleigh	from Ever's meadow	English
Everly	from Ever's meadow	English
Evie	lively	Hebrew
Faith	confidence	Greek
Farrah	happy	Arabic
Fatima	captivating	Arbabic
Faye	fairy	French
Felicity	happiness; good luck	Latin
Fernanda	adventurous	German
Finley	fair hero	Irish
Fiona	white or fair	Gaelic
Frances	free one	Latin
Francesca	free one	Italian
Frankie	free one	French
Freya	lady	Scandinavian
Frida	beautiful	Norse

Gabriela	God's able-bodied one	Hebrew
Gabriella	woman of God	Italian
Gabrielle	woman of God	French
Galilea	a rolled sheet	Italian
Gemma	jewel or gem	Italian
Genesis	beginning	Biblical
Genevieve	of the race of women	German
Georgia	tiller of the soil or farmer	English
Gia	God is gracious	Italian
Giana	God is gracious	Italian
Gianna	God is gracious	Italian
Giavanna	God is kind	Italian
Giovanna	God is kind	Italian
Giselle	pledge	German
Giuliana	young	Italian
Gloria	glory	Latin
Grace	God's favour	English
Gracelyn	combination of Grace and Lyn	American English
Gracelynn	combination of Grace and Lynn	American English
Gracie	favour; blessing	Latin
Greta	pearl	Swedish
Guadalupe	wolf valley	Arabic
Gwen	mythical son of Gwastad	Celtic
Gwendolyn	blessed; white browed	Welsh
Hadassah	myrtle or bride	Persian
Hadlee	heather field	English
Hadleigh	heather field	English
Hadley	heather field	English

Hailee	Hay's meadow	English, Scottish
Hailey	Hay's meadow	English, Scottish
Haley	ingenious	Irish
Halle	little rock	Norse
Hallie	from the Hall	English
Hana	blossom	Japanese
Hanna	grace	Hebrew
Hannah	grace	Hebrew
Harlee	the long field	English
Harley	the long field	English
Harlow	meadow of the hares	English
Harmoni	unity	Latin
Harmony	concord	Latin
Harper	harpist; ministrel	English
Hattie	rules the home	English
Haven	place of shelter; safety	English
Hayden	from the hedged in valley	English
Haylee	hay clearing	English
Hayley	hay field	English
Hazel	hazel tree nut; nut-bearing shrub	English
Heather	a flowering evergreen in Scotland	English
Heaven	heaven	English
Heavenly	little lady	English
Heidi	nobility	French
Helen	the bright one	Greek
Helena	shining light	Greek
Henley	high meadow	English
Holland	wooded land	Dutch

Holly	from the plant name; holy	English
Hope	one of the Christian virtues	English
Hunter	one who hunts	English
Iliana	from Ilium or Troy	Greek
Imani	faith	Arabic
Ingrid	fair; beautiful	Norse
Ireland	place name	English
Irene	peace	Greek
Iris	bringer of joy	Latin
Isabel	my God is beautiful	Latin
Isabela	God of plenty	Spanish
Isabella	devoted to God	Hebrew
Isabelle	devoted to God	Hebrew
Isla	from the name of a Scottish river	Scottish
Itzel	rainbow lady	Mayan
Ivanna	gift from God	Hebrew
Ivory	white; pure	English
Ivy	faithfulness	English
Izabella	devoted to God	Hebrew
Jacqueline	supplanter	French
Jada	knowledgeable one	Hebrew
Jade	jewel	Spanish
Jaelyn	supplanter	American
Jaelynn	supplanter	American
Jaida	the gemstone jade; the color green	English
Jaliyah	no meaning	American
Jamie	supplanter	Hebrew

Jane	Jehovah has been gracious	English
Janelle	God is gracious	English
Janessa	God is gracious	Scottish Norwegian
Janiya	from Jana	Hebrew
Janiyah	from Jana	Hebrew
Jasmin	a flower name; French	
Jasmine	a flower name	Persian
Jaycee	phonetic name based on initials	English
Jayda	knowledgeable one	American Hebrew
Jayde	the color green	English
Jayden	Jehovah has heard	Hebrew
Jayla	to ascend	Hebrew
Jaylah	to ascend	Hebrew
Jaylee	no meaning	American
Jayleen	beautiful jay bird	American
Jaylene	feminine	American
Jaylin	beautiful jay bird	American
Jaylynn	feminine	English
Jazlyn	combination of Jocelyn and the musical term jazz	English
Jazlynn	combination of Jocelyn and musical term jazz	English
Jazmin	flower name	Persian
Jazmine	flower name	Persian
Jemma	dove	Hebrew

Jenna	white shadow; white wave	English
Jennifer	fair one	Arthurian Legend
Jenny	God has been gracious	English
Jessa	short form of Jessica	Hebrew
Jessica	rich	Hebrew
Jessie	wealthy	Hebrew
Jewel	jewel	French
Jillian	child of the gods	English
Jimena	heard	Spanish
Joanna	God is gracious	Latin
Jocelyn	one of the Goths	German
Jocelynn	medieval name adopted as a feminine name	French
Johanna	gift from God	Hebrew
Jolene	compound of Jo and feminine name element −ene	English
Jolie	cheerful	French
Jordan	the river of judgement	Biblical
Jordyn	descend	American
Jordynn	descend	American
Joselyn	member of the Gauts tribe	German
Josephine	may Jehovah add	French
Josie	may Jehovah add	French
Joslyn	medieval male name adopted as feminine name	French
Journee	trip	American
Journey	trip	American

Joy	rejoicing	French
Joyce	cheerful	English
Judith	jewess	Hebrew
Julia	young	Latin
Juliana	youthful	Latin
Julianna	young; Jove's child	Latin
Julianne	downy grace	Latin
Julie	downy	French
Juliet	youthful	French
Julieta	from Julian; Jove's child	Spanish
Juliette	youthful	French
Julissa	descended from Jove	French
June	young	Latin
Juniper	an evergreen tree	English
Latin		
Justice	upright; righteous	Latin
Kadence	falling; rhythm and flow	American, English
Kaelyn	keeper of the keys; pure	American
Kaelynn	keeper of the keys; pure	English
Kai	the sea	Hawiian
Kaia	the sea	Hawiian
Kailani	sea and sky	Hawaiian
Kailee	keeper of the keys; pure	English
Kailey	keeper of the keys; pure	English
Kailyn	pure; English	
Kairi	sea	American

Kaitlyn	form of Caitlin from Catherine meaning pure	Irish
Kaitlynn	form of Caitlin from Catherine meaning pure	Irish
Kaiya	forgiveness	Japanese
Kalani	the sky; cheiftain	Hawaiian
Kali	black	Indian
Kaliyah	ornament; bright one	African American
Kallie	from the forest	Irish
Kamila	perfect	Arabic
Kamryn	modernused for girls	English
Kara	dear; beloved	Italian
Karen	pure	Greek
Karina	pure	English
Karla	womanly; strength	Scandinavian
Karlee	womanly; strength	German
Karlie	womanly	Scandinavian
Karsyn	son of the marsh dwellers	Scottish, Irish
Karter	one who transports goods in a cart	English
Kassandra	unheeded prophetess	Greek
Kassidy	curly-headed	English
Katalina	pure	Greek
Kate	pure; clear	Latin
Katelyn	pure	English
Katelynn	pure	English
Katherine	pure	Latin
Kathleen	pure	Greek
Kathryn	clear; pure	Latin

Katie	pure; clear	Irish
Kaya	my elder sister	Native American, Hopi
Kayden	son of Caden; battle	English
Kaydence	falling; rhythm	American English
Kayla	keeper of the keys; pure	English
Kaylee	pure	English
Kayleigh	pure; keeper of the keys	English
Kaylie	keeper of the keys; pure	English
Kaylin	keeper of the keys; pure	English
Kaylynn	keeper of the keys; pure	English
Keira	dusky; dark-haired	Irish
Kelly	war; lively	Irish
Kelsey	from the ship's land	Norse
Kendall	royal valley	English
Kendra	knowledge	English
Kenia	form of Kenya	Hebrew
Kenley	from the king's meadow	English
Kenna	born of fire	Scottish
Kennedi	misshapen head	Irish
Kennedy	helmeted	Irish
Kensington	the town of Cynsige's People	English
Kensley	spring glade	English, Nordic
Kenya	yes to God	Hebrew

Kenzie	good-looking	American, Scottish
Keyla	pure; English	
Khaleesi	modern invented name	American
Khloe	young green shoot	English
Kiana	ancient	Irish
Kiara	dark	Irish
Kiera	dark-haired	Irish
Kiley	a wood or church	Gaelic
Kimber	royal fortress	Anglo-Saxon
Kimberly	from the wood of the royal forest	English
Kimora	brave and noble	Japanese
Kinley	fair skinned warrior	Gaelic Scottish
Kinslee	land of the king	English
Kinsley	king's field	English
Kira	light	Russian
Kora	maiden	Greek
Kori	God's peace; spear Gaelic	Germanic Celtic
Kristen	follower of Cgrist	Latin
Kristina	Follower of Christ	Latin
Kyla	feminine of Kyle	Gaelic
Kylee	feminine of Kyle	Gaelic
Kyleigh	feminine of Kyle	Gaeilc
Kylie	feminine of Kyle	Gaelic
Kyndall	royal valley	English
Kynlee	respelling of Kinley	American
Kyra	enthroned	Greek
Lacey	surname	Irish
Laila	born at night	Arabic

Lailah	born at night; sweetheart	Muslim
Lainey Welsh	ray of light	English
Lana	derived from Irish Gaelic word for child	Gaelic
Landry	ruler	Anglo-Saxon
Laney	path; roadway	English
Lara	cheerful	Russian
Laura	laurel tree or sweet bay tree	Latin
Laurel	laurel	Latin, American
Lauren	of Laurentum	Latin
Lauryn	from Laurentum	Latin
Layla	born at night	Egyptian
Laylah	night; nocturnal	Arabic
Lea	derived from Hebrew Leah	Spanish
Leah	tired	Hebrew
Leanna	derived from an Irish Gaelic of Helen	English
Leia	child of heaven; heavenly flowers	Hawaiian
Leighton	her garden	English
Leila	born at night	Persian
Leilani	heavenly flower	Hawaiian
Lena	temptress	Russian
Lennon	little cloak	Gaelic
Lennox	lives near the place abounding in elm trees	Gaelic
Leona	lioness	French

Leslie	Scottish surname and place name	Scottish
Lexi	man's defender	Greek
Lexie	man's defender	Greek
Leyla	born at night	Arabic
Lia	bearer of good news; dependent	Greek, Hebrew, Italian
Liana	youthful	Latin
Libby	God's promise	English
Liberty	free	American
Lila	lilac; born at night	Persian
Lilah	feminine of Lyle: from the island	English
Lilia	purity and beauty	Latin
Lilian	derived from the flower name Lily; innocence	English
Liliana	lily	American
Lilianna	innocence; purity	Latin
Lilith	night monster	Hebrew
Lillian	innocence and beauty	English
Lilliana	purity; beauty	Latin
Lillianna	purity; beauty	Latin
Lillie	innocence; purtiy	English
Lilly	purity; beauty	English
Lily	pure; English	
Lilyana	God is my oath	English
Lilyanna	combination of Lily and Anna	English
Lina	tender	Muslim
Linda	snake; lime tree	German

Lindsay	from the island of the lime tree	Scottish
Lindsey	from the island of the lime tree	Scottish
Lisa	oath of God	Hebrew
Liv	life	Scandinavian
Livia	life	English
Lizbeth	oath of God	Hebrew
Logan	from the hollow	Gaelic
Lola	sorrow	Spanish
London	place name	English
Londyn	respelling of London	Celtic
Lorelai	temptress	German
Lorelei	temptress	German
Louisa	famous warrior	Latin
Lucia	graceful light	Italian
Luciana	light	Latin
Lucille	French light	French
Lucy	light	Latin
Luna	the moon	Latin
Luz	seperation; an almond	Biblical
Lydia	woman from Lydia	Greek
Lyla	from the island	English
Lylah	amusement; dark beauty	American, Arabic, English
Lyra	lyre; lyrical	Greek
Lyric	of the lyre; song	French
Mabel	beautiful; lovable	Latin
Maci	derived from medieval form of Matthew	English
Macie	derived from medieval form of Matthew	English

Mackenzie	fair; favoured one	Scottish
Macy	derived from medieval male form of Matthew	French
Madalyn	from the tower	Hebrew
Madalynn	bitter	Spanish
Maddison	mighty battle	English
Madeleine	woman of Magdala	French
Madeline	woman of Magdala	French
Madelyn	high tower	Greek
Madelynn	high tower	Greek
Madilyn	high tower	Greek
Madilynn	high tower	Greek
Madison	derived from Matthew 'gift of God'	English
Madisyn	derived from Matthew 'gift of God'	English
Madyson	derived from Matthew ' gift of God'	English
Mae	May	French
Maeve	joy	Irish
Maggie	pearl	Greek
Magnolia	flower	French
Maia	May	French
Maisie	pearl' child of light	Scottish
Makayla	who is like God	English
Makenna	happy one	Eastern African
Makenzie	comely; good-looking	Celtic, Gaelic, Scottish
Malaya	free	Filipino
Malaysia	land of mountains	American
Maleah	bitter	Hawaiian
Malia	bitter	Hawaiian

Maliah	bitter	Hawaiian
Maliyah	bitter	Hawaiian
Mallory	unfortunate; ill fated	French
Mara	bitter	English
Margaret	pearl	Greek
Margot	pearl	French
Maria	rebellion	Latin
Mariah	bitter	English
Mariam	bitter	Arabic
Mariana	bitter	Latin
Marianna	bitter	Latin
Marie	rebellion; wished for-child	Hebrew
Marilyn	rebillion; bitter	Hebrew
Marina	from the sea	Latin
Marisol	Mary soledad; Mary alone	Latin
Marissa	of the sea	Latin
Mariyah	the Lord is my teacher	Latin
Marjorie	pearl	Greek
Marlee	pleasant seaside meadow	English
Marleigh	pleasant seaside meadow	English
Marley	pleasant seaside meadow	English
Martha	lady	Aramaic
Mary	wished-for child; rebellion	Hebrew
Maryam	bitter	Greek
Matilda	strength in battle	German
Maya	daughter of Atlas	Latin

Mckenna	beloved of Aodh(Celtic god of fire)	Celtic, Gaelic, Irish
Mckenzie	the fair one	Scottish
Mckinley	son of the white warrior; learned ruler	Gaelic
Meadow	grassy field	American
Megan	pearl	Greek
Meilani	heavenly beautiful	Hawaiian
Melanie	the black one	Latin
Melany	the black one	Latin
Melina	honey	Greek
Melissa	bee	Greek
Melody	music	Greek
Meredith	guardian of the sea	Welsh
Mia	commonly-used; wished-for child	Latin
Miah	mine; bitter	Swedish
Micah	gift from God	Hebrew
Michaela	gift from God	English
Michelle	close to God	Hebrew
Mikaela	gift from God	English
Mikayla	gift from God	English
Mila	industrious	Czechoslovakian
Milan	gracious	Slavic
Milana	gracious	Slavic
Milani	from Milan	Italian
Milania	gracious	Greek
Milena	people's love	Russian
Millie	mild of strength	English
Mina	love	German
Mira	worthy of admiration; wonderful	Latin

Miracle	wonder	Latin
Miranda	wonderful	Latin
Miriam	rebellious	Hebrew
Miya	three arrows; temple	Japanese
Molly	bitter	English
Monica	alone; advisor	Greek
Monroe	from the red swamp	Gaelic
Monserrat	a mountain in Spain	Latin
Montserrat	jagged mountain	American
Morgan	bright sea	Welsh
Moriah	the Lord is my teacher	Hebrew
Mya	beloved	Egyptian
Myah	water	Greek
Myla	merciful	English
Myra	pour out; weep	Biblical
Nadia	hope	Slavic
Nala	olive	Latin
Nancy	grace	Hebrew
Naomi	pleasant	Hebrew
Natalee	birthday; especially birthday of Christ	French
Natalia	born at Christmas	Russian
Natalie	born at Christmas	French
Nataly	born at Christmas	French
Natasha	born at Christmas	Russian
Nathalia	birthday; especially birthday of Christ	French
Nathalie	birthday; especially birthday of Christ	French
Nathaly	birthday; especially birthday of Christ	French
Naya	brilliance	Swahili

Nayeli	I love you	Zapotec
Neriah	light; lamp of the Lord	Biblical
Nevaeh	heaven spelled backwards	American
Nia	brilliance	Swahili
Nicole	people's victory	Greek
Nina	favour grace	English
Noa	movement	Hebrew
Noelle	birthday	French
Noemi	pleasantness	Spanish
Nola	feminine of Nolan(noble)	Gaelic
Noor	light	Arabic
Nora	abbreviation of Ealeanora 'light' and Honora 'honor'	English
Norah	honour	Latin
Nova	new; young	Latin
Nyla	winner	African America, Arabic
Nylah	winner	African American, Arabic
Oakley	from the oak-tree meadow	English
Olive	symbol of peace	Latin
Olivia	olive branch	Latin
Ophelia	hemp; serpentine	Greek
Paige	attendant	French
Paislee	church; cemetery	English
Paisley	church cemetery	Scottish
Paityn	fighting man's estate	English
Paloma	dove	Spanish

Paola	small	Latin
Paris	place name	Greek
Parker	keeper of the forest	English
Patricia	regal; noble	Latin
Paula	small	Latin
Paulina	small	Latin
Payton	fighting man's estate	English
Pearl	precious	Latin
Penelope	bobbin	Greek
Penny	flower; bobbin	Greek
Perla	precious	Spanish
Peyton	fighting man's estate	English
Phoebe	the shining one	Greek
Phoenix	bird reborn from its own ashes	Greek
Piper	piper	English
Presley	from the priest's meadow	English
Princess	royal son	American
Priscilla	ancient	Latin
Quinn	counsel	Gaelic
Rachel	ewe	Hebrew
Raegan	impulsive	Irish
Raelyn	well advised protector	American
Raelynn	well advised protector	American
Raina	queen	French
Raquel	innocent	Hebrew
Raven	raven	English
Rayna	queen	Hebrew
Reagan	regal	Celtic
Rebecca	captivating; knotted cord	Hebrew

Rebekah	captivating; knotted cord	Hebrew
Reese	ardent; fiery	Welsh
Regina	queen	Spanish
Reina	queen	Spanish
Remi	rower	French
Remington	from the raven farm	English
Remy	rower	French
Renata	reborn	Latin
Reyna	queen	Spanish
Rhea	the mother of the Greek god Zues	Greek
Riley	surname	Irish
River	riverbank	Latin
Rivka	captivating	Hebrew
Romina	from the land of the Christians	Arabic
Rory	red	Irish
Rosa	rose	Italian
Rosalie	rose	Latin
Rose	flower	Scottish
Roselyn	red haired	French
Rosemary	bitter rose	Latin
Rosie	rose	Latin
Rowan	red	Gaelic
Royal	red	Gaelic
Ruby	precious jewel	Latin
Ruth	companion	Hebrew
Ryan	kingly	Irish
Ryann	little king	Irish
Rylan	island meadow	Irish
Rylee	couageous	Irish

Ryleigh	courageous	Irish
Rylie	courageous	Irish
Sabrina	from Cyprus or from the river Severn	Latin
Sadie	mercy	Spanish
Sage	wise one	English
Saige	wise one	English
Salma	peace; perfection	Biblical
Samantha	listener	Aramaic
Samara	protected by God	Hebrew
Sandra	defender of men	Greek
Saniyah	radiant	Arabic
Sara	princess	Hebrew
Sarah	princess	Hebrew
Sarahi	my princess	Hebrew
Sarai	my lady	Biblical
Sariah	my lady	Biblical
Sariyah	my lady	Biblical
Sasha	defender of men	Russian
Savanna	from the open plain	Spanish
Savannah	from the open plain	Spanish
Sawyer	cuts timber	Celtic
Saylor	rope maker	Germanic
Scarlet	red	English
Scarlett	red	English
Scarlette	red	English
Selah	to praise	Hebrew
Selena	moon goddess	Greek
Serena	serene	Italian
Serenity	serene; calm	French
Sharon	from the Plain of Sharon	Hebrew
Shayla	question	Hebrew

Shelby	from the manor house 'Willow farm'	English
Shiloh	the one to whom it belongs	Hebrew
Sidney	wide island	English
Siena	from Siena	Latin
Sienna	name of a city in Italy	Italian
Sierra	dark	Irish
Simone	heard	French
Sky	cloud	Norse
Skye	Isle of Skye	English
Skyla	sheltering	Dutch
Skylar	phonetic spelling of Schuyler	English
Skyler	phonetic spelling of Schuyler	English
Sloan	warrior	Gaelic
Sloane	warrior	Gaelic
Sofia	wise	Greek
Sophia	wise	Greek
Sophie	wise	Greek
Stella	derived from 'stella' meaning star	French
Stephanie	crown; victorious	Greek
Stevie	victorious	Greek
Summer	born during the summer	English
Susan	graceful lily	Hebrew
Sutton	from the south farm	English
Sydney	from Saint-Denis	French
Sylvia	from the forest	Latin
Tabitha	beauty; grace	Hebrew

Talia	dew of heaven	Hebrew
Taliyah	dew of heaven	Hebrew
Tara	where the kings met	Irish
Tatiana	feminine of Roman family clan name Tatius	Russian
Tatum	brings joy	English
Taya	valley field	Japanese
Taylor	tailor	English
Teagan	good-looking	Irish
Tegan	good-looking	Irish
Tenley	town	English
Teresa	name of saints 'Teresa of Avila' and 'Teresa of Lisieux'	Spanish
Tessa	born fourth	Greek
Thalia	joyous muse of comedy	Greek
Thea	goddess	Greek
Tiana	uncertain	English
Tiffany	manifestation of God	Latin
Tinley	hedge; fence	English
Tori	triumphant	English
Trinity	three in one	Latin
Valentina	brave	Latin
Valeria	brave	Latin
Valerie	brave	Latin
Vanessa	butterfly	Greek
Veda	understanding	Sanskrit
Wendy	literary	English
Vera	faith; true	Russian
Veronica	true image	Latin
Whitney	from the white island	Anglo-Saxon

Victoria	victory; triumphant	Latin
Vienna	from Wine Country	American
Willa	valiant protector	English
Willow	slender; graceful	English
Winter	year	Anglo-Saxon
Violet	flower	Italian
Virginia	virgin	Spanish
Vivian	lively	Latin
Viviana	enchantress of Merlin	Latin
Vivienne	lively	French
Wren	ruler	Welsh
Wynter	born in the winter	English
Ximena	one who hears	Spanish
Yamileth	beautiful	Spanish
Yareli	lady of the water	Spanish
Yaretzi	you will always be loved	Aztec
Yaritza	water lady	Spanish
Yasmin	jasmine flower	Arabic
Zahra	white	Arabic
Zainab	daughter of the Prophet Muhammad	Muslim
Zaniyah	forever always	Aztec
Zara	Eastern splendour; princess	Arabic
Zaria	flower or sunrise	Arabic
Zariah	blooming flower or sunrise	Arabic
Zariyah	flower or sunrise	Arabic
Zaylee	flower	Australian
Zelda	grey battle; Christian battle	German

Zendaya	give thanks	Shona
Zion	monument; raised up	Biblical
Zoe	life; alive	Greek
Zoey	life	Greek
Zoie	life	Greek
Zuri	white and lovely	French

Chapter 3

The Most Popular Girl Names

Eliana	My God has answered	Hebrew
Victoria	Victory	Latin
Faith	Belief, To trust	English
Harper	Harp player	English
Mila	Diminutive of several European names	Slavic
Penelope	Weaver	Greek
Olivia	Olive tree	Latin
Bella	Beautiful	Latin
Stella	Star	Latin
Autumn	Autumn	Latin
Allison	Noble	German
Eva	Life	Hebrew
Violet	Purple	Latin
Kaylee	Laurel, Crown	Celtic
Lily	flower name	English
Alyssa	Noble	German
Savannah	Flat tropical grassland	English
Madeline	Women from Magdala or high tower	Hebrew
Emilia	Rival; emulating (Latin). Industrious (Germanic). Friendly; soft (Greek).	Latin

Name	Meaning	Origin
Ashley	Dweller near the ash tree meadow	English
Grace	Grace of God, Beauty of form	Latin
Natalie	Birthday of the Lord	Latin
Maya	Water	Sanskrit
Hazel	The hazelnut tree	English
Lucy	Light	Latin
Emma	Universal	Latin
Trinity	Triad	English
Skylar	Guarded, learned one (American). Eternal life and strength (English)	Dutch
Emily	Rival	Latin
Lydia	Women from Lydia	Greek
Willow	the Willow tree	English
Katherine	Pure	Greek
Alice	Noble	German
Liliana	To climb, like a vine	English
Julia	Youthful	Latin
Hailey	Hay's meadow	English
Ruby	Deep red precious stone	Latin
Layla	Night	Arabic
Audrey	Noble strength	German
Aaliyah	Heavens, Exalted, Highborn	Hebrew
Sadie	Princess	Hebrew
Lillian	Lily, A Flower	Hebrew
Alexa	Defending men	Greek
Nora	Light	Latin
Camila	Young ceremonial attendant	French

Ella	Fairy maiden, All, Completly	French
Jasmine	Persian flower name	Persian
Hannah	Grace	Hebrew
Brianna	Strong, honorable and virtuous	Celtic
Kylie	A boomerang	Celtic
Amelia	Work	Hebrew
Aria	Air, Lioness	Latin
Brooklyn	Place-name	English
Jade	Stone of the side	Spanish
Serenity	Peaceful	Latin
Adeline	Noble, Nobility	English
Aubree	Elf ruler	French
Zoey	Life	Greek
Paisley	Church, cemetery	Gaelic
Isabella	Pledged to God	Hebrew
Anna	Grace	Hebrew
Natalia	Birthday of the Lord	Latin
Nevaeh	Modern invented name	English
Claire	Clear, bright	Latin
Leah	Weary	Hebrew
Valentina	Health, Strenght	Latin
Madelyn	High tower or women from Magdala	Hebrew
Madison	Son of Maud	English
Scarlett	Red	English
Sofia	Wisdom	Greek
Abigail	My father is joyful	Hebrew
Eleanor	Pity (Greek). God is my light (Arabic	Hebrew
Delilah	To flirt	Hebrew

Aurora	Dawn	Latin
Annabelle	Loving	Italian
Elena	Shining light, bright	Greek
Naomi	Pleasantness	Hebrew
Evelyn	Wished for child	Celtic
Ava	Life	Hebrew
Melanie	Dark, Black	Greek
Alexis	Defender	Greek
Piper	Flute player or piper	English
Isabelle	Pledged to God	Hebrew
Sarah	Princess	Hebrew
Ariana	Most holy	Welsh
Samantha	Told by God	English
Zoe	Life	Greek
Adalynn	Noble guardian	English
Arianna	the Very holy one	Greek
Mia	Mine; bitter	Latin
Chloe	Young green shoot	Greek
Sophia	Wisdom	Greek
Gabriella	God is my strength	Italian
Gianna	The Lord is gracious	Hebrew
Caroline	Freeman	German
Luna	Moon	Latin
Charlotte	Freeman	Norse
Ellie	Shining one, Bright	Hebrew
Athena	Greek Goddess of wisdom	Greek
Elizabeth	Pledged to God	Hebrew

Chapter 4

The Most Popular Boy Names

Name	Meaning	Origin
Aaron	High mountain; enlightened, exalted	Hebrew
Adam	Son of the red earth	Hebrew
Adrian	Man of Adria	Latin
Aiden	Fiery and little	Celtic
Alexander	Defending men	Greek
Andrew	Manly and strong	Greek
Angel	Word name	Greek
Anthony	Priceless one	English
Asher	Happy one, Fortunate, Blessed	Hebrew
Austin	Magnificent, Great	Latin
Ayden	Little fire	Celtic
Benjamin	son of the right hand	Hebrew
Bentley	Meadow with coarse grass	English
Brandon	Broom-covered hill	English
Brayden	Broad hill	Celtic
Bryson	Son of Brice	Welsh
Caleb	Devotion to God	Hebrew
Cameron	Bent nose	Celtic
Carson	Son of the marsh dwellers	Celtic

Carter	Driver or cart maker	English
Charles	Freeman	German
Chase	To hunt	English
Christian	Follower of Christ	Latin
Christopher	Bearer of Christ	Greek
Colton	From the coal or dark town	English
Connor	Lover of hounds	Celtic
Cooper	Barrel maker	English
Daniel	God is my judge	Hebrew
David	Beloved	Hebrew
Dominic	Belonging to the lord	Latin
Dylan	Son of the sea	Welsh
Easton	East facing place	English
Eli	Ascended, high	Hebrew
Elias	My God is the lord	Hebrew
Elijah	Yahweh is God	Hebrew
Ethan	Firm, strong	Hebrew
Evan	The Lord is gracious	Hebrew
Ezra	Helper	Hebrew
Gabriel	God is my strength	Hebrew
Gavin	White hawk	Welsh
Grayson	The son of the bailiff	English
Greyson	Son of the steward	English
Henry	Estate ruler	German
Hudson	Son of Hugh	English
Hunter	One who hunts	English
Ian	The Lord is gracious	Hebrew
Isaac	Laughter	Hebrew
Isaiah	Salvation of the Lord	Hebrew
Jace	Moon-Var. of Jason	Greek
Jack	God is gracious	English
Jackson	Son of Jack	English
Jacob	Supplanter	Hebrew

James	Supplanter	Hebrew
Jason	To heal	Greek
Jaxon	Jack's son	Greek
Jaxson	Jack's son	English
Jayden	God has heard	Hebrew
Jeremiah	Appointed by God	Hebrew
John	God is gracious	Hebrew
Jonathan	Gift of Jehovah	Hebrew
Jordan	Flowing down	Hebrew
Jose	Jehovah increases	Spanish
Joseph	Jehovah increases	Hebrew
Joshua	The Lord is my salvation	Hebrew
Josiah	Heals, God supports	Hebrew
Julian	Downy, Youthful	Latin
Kayden	Battle, Son of Cadan	Celtic
Kevin	Handsome	Celtic
Landon	Long hill	English
Leo	Lion	Latin
Leonardo	Brave lion	German
Levi	Attached, joined	Hebrew
Liam	Resolute protection	German
Lincoln	Town by the pool	English
Logan	Little hollow	Celtic
Lucas	Man from Luciana	Latin
Luke	Man from Luciana	Greek
Mason	Stoneworker	French
Mateo	Gift of God	Hebrew
Matthew	Gift of God	Hebrew
Michael	Who is like God?	Hebrew
Nathan	Given	Hebrew
Nicholas	People of Victory	Greek
Noah	Comfort, Rest	Hebrew
Nolan	Champion	Celtic

Oliver	Olive tree	German
Owen	Well-born; young warrior	Welsh
Parker	Park keeper	French
Robert	Bright fame	German
Roman	Citizen of Rome	Latin
Ryan	Little king	Celtic
Samuel	Told by God	Hebrew
Santiago	Saint James	Latin
Sebastian	From the ancient city of Sebasta	German
Thomas	Twin	Aramaic
Tyler	Maker of tiles	English
William	Resolute protection	German
Wyatt	Brave in war	English
Xavier	Bright or new house	Basque
Zachary	The Lord has remembered	Hebrew
Marques		Portuguese, Spanish
Manzie		American
Manny		English, Spanish
Manning		English
Manley		English
Manfred		English, Teutonic
Macleod		Gaelic, English
Mackean		Scottish
Lenno		Native American
Karl		German, Teutonic
Kale		Hawaiian
Jove		Greek, Latin

Jerry	English, German, Greek
Jermaine	Latin
Jarvis	Old English, German, English
Janus	Latin
Ibrahim	Hebrew, Arabic
Howard	Old English, English
Gregory	Latin, Greek
Gregor	Dutch, Greek
German	French, English, Spanish
Germaine	French
Gerardo	German, Spanish
Gerard	English, Teutonic
Gavrie	Russian
Gatlin	English
Garrett	Old German, Irish, English
Freeman	English
Francesco	Italian, Latin
Foster	English
Forsythe	Gaelic
Flynn	Irish, Celtic
Fisher	Old English, English
Fabrizio	Italian
Fabrice	Italian
Eugenie	Greek
Eugene	Greek
Ellsworth	English Hebrew

Edgar	Old English, English
Earl	Old English, Celtic
Duke	French, English
Destry	English, French
Desmond	Irish, Gaelic, Celtic
Dermot	Irish, Celtic
Declan	Gaelic, Irish, Celtic
Charles	Old German, German, Teutonic
Cartman	English
Carl	Teutonic, Old German, German, English
Bwana	Swahili
Butch	American
Bono	Latin
Bolton	English
Armando	German, Spanish, Teutonic
Armand	German, Teutonic
Archer	English
Apollo	Greek
Ansel	German, French
Andrew	Greek
Andreas	Greek, Teutonic

Anders	Scandinavian, Greek
Almanzo	Old German
Alexander	Greek
Adam	Hebrew
Abraham	Hebrew
Marquis	French
Medgar	German
Oscar	Old English, Scandinavian, English
Paine	Latin
Patrick	Latin
Pompey	Latin
Quenby	Scandinavian
Quimby	Scandinavian
Richard	Old German, English
Rodman	German, English
Roger	Old German, German, English
Romany	Romany
Rutger	Scandinavian, Dutch
Ryder	Old English, English
Saxon	English
Steadman	English
Thurgood	English
Truman	English
Wayman	English
Wentworth	English

Whit	English
Whitman	English
Yancey	Native American

Chapter 5

Trending Names

These are some of the most popular baby names, as compiled by Baby Center.

Girls:

Emma	Harper
Olivia	Aria
Ava	Ella
Sophia	Abigail
Mia	Evelyn
Charlotte	Chloe

Boys:

Liam	Jackson
Noah	Logan
Lucas	Ethan
Mason	Aidan
Oliver	Elijah
Benjamin	Michael

International Names

Key: Name (Origin)   Meaning

Name (Origin)	Meaning
Aiden (Irish)	Litte and fiery
Alden (English)	Wise, old friend
Alexander (Greek)	Defender
Amos (Hebrew)	Carried by God
Andrew (Greek)	Manly, Strong
Benjamin (Hebrew)	Son of the right hand
Booker (English)	Scribe
Caleb (Hebrew)	Dog (faithful, loyal)
Carter (English)	Transporter of goods
Charles (French)	Freeman
Christopher	(Greek, Christ, bearer, Latin)
Daniel (Hebrew)	"God is my judge."
David (Hebrew)	Beloved
Dylan (Welsh)	Son of the sea
Elijah (Hebrew)	"God is my salvation."
Ethan (Hebrew)	Strong, firm
Forrest (English)	Forest
Gabriel (Hebrew)	"God is my strength."
Gideon (Hebrew)	Hewer
Grayson (English)	Son of the bailiff
Hunter (English)	One who hunts
Isaiah (Hebrew)	Salvation of the Lord
Isaac (Hebrew)	Laughter
Jackson, Jaxon (English)	Son of Jack
James (Hebrew)	Variation of Jacob
Jacob (Hebrew)	Heel grabber, a deceiver
Joseph (Hebrew)	"Jehovah increases."
Josiah (Hebrew)	"God supports, heals."

Jonathan (Hebrew)	"Gift of Jehovah"
Julian (Latin)	Downy
Landon (English)	Long hill
Levi (Hebrew)	Joined, attached
Liam (Irish), William (English, German)	Resolute protection
Logan (Scottish)	Small Hollow
Lucas, Luke (Latin)	From Lucania
Mason (English)	Worker in stone
Matthew (Hebrew)	Gift of God
Michael (Hebrew)	"Who is like God?"
Nathan (Hebrew)	Given
Noah (Hebrew)	Rest, wandering
Oliver (Latin)	Olive tree
Reeve (English)	Baliff
Ryan (Irish)	Little king
Samuel (Hebrew)	Told by God
Sebastian (Latin, Greek)	from Sebasta
William (English, German)	Resolute protection
Winston (English)	Of the town of wine
Wyatt (English)	Brave warrior

List of Popular Names for Girls in the United States

Key: Name (Origin)   **Meaning**

Aaliyah (Arabic)	Exalted
Abigail (Hebrew)	"My father is joyful."
Addison (English)	Son of Adam
Alexa (Greek)	Defender
Allison (Scottish)	Noble

Amelia (German)	Work
Aria (Hebrew)	Air, Song
Ariana (Italian) Variation of Ariadne	Most Holy
Aubrey (English, French, German)	Elf ruler
Audrey (English)	Noble strength
Aurora (Latin)	Dawn
Ava, Eva (Latin)	Life
Avery (English)	Elf ruler
Bella (Italian)	Beautiful
Brooklyn (English)	Stream
Camilla (Latin)	Ceremonial assistant
Charlotte (French)	Free
Chloe (Greek)	Sprout
Ella (English)	Light, Beautiful fairy
Elizabeth (Hebrew)	Pledged to God
Emma (German)	Universal
Emily (Latin) Variation of Emil	Rival
Evelyn (French) Variation of Aveline	Wished for child
Hannah (Hebrew)	Grace
Harper (English)	Harp player
Grace	
Isabella (Spanish, Italian) Variation of Elizabeth	Pledged to God
Layla (Arabic)	Night
Leah (Hebrew)	Weary
Lillian (English, Latin) Lily	Flower
Luna (Latin)	Moon
Madison (English)	Son of Maud

Maya (Hebrew)	Water
Mia (Italian)	Mine
Mila	Diminutive of several European names
Natalie (French)	Birthday of the Lord
Nevaeh (English)	Spelling variation of "heaven"
Olivia (Latin)	Olive Tree
Penelope (Greek)	Weaver
Riley (Irish)	Courageous
Sadie-Diminutive of Sarah (Hebrew)	Princess
Samantha (Hebrew) Feminine for Samuel	Told by God
Savannah (Spanish)	Flat, tropical grassland
Scarlett (English)	Red
Skylar-Variation on Schuyler	Scholar
Sophia (Greek)	Wisdom
Victoria (Latin)	Victory
Zoey (Greek)	Life

Chapter 6

Inspiring Baby Names from Hindu

Baby Boy Names

It seems that Hindus come up with the most interesting names. Their respective Sanskrit meaning adds more depth to the names. Each name represents virtue and value. If you want a spiritual start for your bundle of joy, consider the following baby boy names based in Hinduism.

ABHAS [AH-bahs]

This is a Sanskrit name which means "awareness or realization." Abhas is inspirational and creative. He strives to achieve harmony within himself. He is a loving and caring person who does not hesitate to help others. Outgoing and friendly, Abhas makes friends easily.

AADIR [AH-deer]

Indian by origin, this Hindi name means "beginning or origin." It signifies a source. Aadir is a source of unity and harmony. He is a peacemaker. Reliable, responsible and consistent, he is someone who makes other people feel secure. He treats his loved ones with respect and devotion. Aadir has set clear goals and takes actions guided by his vision of the future.

AADRIK [AHD-reek]

Telugu by origin, Aadrik is the "rising sun between the mountains." He is indeed a symbol of hope and harmony. He is excellent in bridging gaps. Compassionate and protective of others, Aadrik's devotion is unquestionable. He is someone who is dedicated to his work and is likely to accomplish something significant.

AAGAR [AH-guhr]

In Sanskrit, the name refers to someone who is musically inclined. Aagar does not fall short in creativity and inspiration. He is filled with confidence, blessed with wisdom and spirituality. He is someone who takes initiative for others to follow. Outgoing and sociable, he builds friendship easily.

AANAND [AH-nand]

In Sanskrit, this Hindu name is a symbol of good fortune. It signifies delight, happiness and bliss. A gift to the community, Aanand is socially active and born leader. He is guided by his passion. Adventurous in spirit, he is an explorer. While he enjoys his freedom, he does not forget his responsibilities. He works hard to be able to succeed in his life.

ABHAI [AHB-bhay]

Abhai means "fearless." He has a deep sense of purpose. This motivates him to work hard. He tackles life with great enthusiasm. His positivity is an inspiration to others. Dynamic, devoted and capable, Abhai is able to bring forth the best in people.

ABHAIVEER [AH-bay-veer]

Sikh by origin, this name refers to someone "who is bold and brave." Born with an adventurous spirit, Abhaiveer does not let anything hold him back. He likes to explore and experience new things. He is passionate and socially active. With a knack for creativity, he inspires others. He is hardworking and will stop at nothing until he succeeds.

ABHATA [AH-buh-tah]

In Sanskrit, Abhata is synonymous to shining and glorious, blazing and splendid. He is admirable in his creative thinking. He shines socially as a natural entertainer. He is a stand out with his social, outgoing and friendly personality. His love and care for his loved ones are unwarranted.

AINESH [AY-nesh]

Of Indian origin, Ainesh means "sun's glory." His passions are as bright as the sun. His adventurous spirit is blinding. His insights and ideas are always grand. His art and creativity are unyielding. And he does splendid things with his generous heart.

AIVANNAN [AY-vahn-nuhn]

Aivannan is one of Lord Shiva's name in Tamil. Aivannan is moved with a purpose in mind. His creative approach to things allows him to come up with innovative ideas. He is dynamic and efficient at work. An inspirational character, he has the ability to motivate people.

BHUDHARA [BOOHD-hah-ruh]

Its Indian roots suggest a link to Lord Krishna. The name itself means "supporter of the earth." Reliable support to others, Bhudhara has a sense of duty. Other people find him trustworthy because of his reliability and consistency. He lives a life of kindness and generosity. He finds happiness in being able to help others. His versatility and remarkable enthusiasm allow him to overcome challenges that may come his way.

BIJENDER [bee-JEHN-der]

This Hindu name is synonymous to courage. With a brave spirit, Bijender takes the initiative and leads. He is capable of handling responsibilities. He fulfills his duties with precision. He recognizes opportunities when they come his way. He is independent and he calls the shots in his life.

CATAKA [KAH-tuh-kah]

From India, this name refers to someone "which is a poet." Cataka's wisdom and spirituality along with his ability for keen observation allow him to have a deep understanding of people and situations. Although he may be introverted, he is intelligent and confident about his skills. He possesses inspired creativity. When given a chance, Cataka can prove himself to be a worthy leader.

DEEPIKA [deeh-PEEH-kuh]

Of Indian origin, this Hindu name means "sun's light" or "lord of heat." Deepika's warmth can be felt through his deep love and caring for his loved ones. He is devoted, generous and self-sacrificing. He has a way of making people feel at ease. He holds a strong sense of duty.

DEESHAN [DEEH-shahn| DEY-shan]

This Hindu name refers to "someone who shows direction." Born with leadership skills, Deeshan is likely to take the initiative and be in control. He is also a born diplomat with his ability to bridge gaps. He is idealistic, compassionate and devoted. Naturally charming, he attracts draws people in.

RAAJEEV [rah-JEEV]

Of Indian origin, Raajeev refers to "Blue Lotus." It signifies someone who is an achiever or "one who rules all." A passionate leader, he is active in social matters and he tries to involve others. He is an inspirational character whose creativity is well admired. He strives for success and recognition.

RAAVI [rah-VEE]

Raavi refers to the sun. It signifies brightness and radiance. He shines through his ability to make people trust and feel secure around him. He has a clear vision of his future and makes decisions in the present accordingly. Responsible and consistent with deep patriotism, Raavi is likely to fill an important position in society.

Raavi's genuine concern and sympathy for others make him a natural peacemaker. He is loving and makes sure to look after his loved ones. Charity gives him a sense of inner harmony.

SAADAR [sah-DUHR]

In Sanskrit, Saadar is synonymous to respect. A passionate person with a zest for life, Saadar is respected for his work ethic. He is admired for his highly creative ideas and insights. He is well-liked for his outgoing personality.

SANTOSO [sahn-TOW-sow]

In Sanskrit, this Hindu name means "peaceful." Santoso has a warm presence about him. His personality signifies grace and charm. His idealism, kind heart and compassion, deep understanding, sincerity and honesty makes him well-loved as a leader.

TANSHU [tahn-SHOO]

This Indian name means "wholly natural." Intelligent, introverted and independent, Tanshu seems like a mystery. He embodies wisdom and spirituality. He has a gift of seeing through people and acts with honesty and sincerity. He is responsible and practical which makes him an excellent team player.

VACHASYA [vah-KASH-yuh]

In Sanskrit, the name refers to someone who is "well-spoken of." Vachasya's passion, creativity, leadership, adventurous and inspirational spirit are well celebrated. He is someone who works relentlessly to accomplish something important.

YATHART [YAH-thart]

This Sanskrit name means "truth or complete." A natural peacemaker, Yathart's ability to bring people together is remarkable. He is idealistic and compassionate. He has the marks of a leader. His presence is always welcome. He embodies grace and charm which draws people in. He possesses clarity of mind and contributes innovative ideas.

Baby Girl Names

Hindu inspired baby girl names are like flowers that exude a pleasant smell. More than the lovely sound they create though is a gentle feeling it leaves you as you find out what they mean. They are uniquely beautiful and anyone, including your little pretty darling, will be honored to bear any of these meaningful names.

AABHA [AHB-bah]

From Sanskrit, this Hindu name means "light, brilliance or glow." It also signifies "gloriousness" and "splendor." Aabha exudes her radiance with her outgoing and friendly personality. Her creativity is inspired. Dynamic and capable, she approaches things in a unique way. She upholds a purpose and she uses this as motivation. A responsible individual, Aabha is a capable leader.

AABHARANA [AHB-ha-rah-nah]

This Hindi name refers to valuables like ornaments and jewels. In a deeper sense, it signifies honor, happiness and prosperity. Aabharana is filled with understanding and compassion. She has clarity in her thoughts and is able to come up with great ideas and insights. She brings honor to her name by living a life of generosity. To her family, she is protective and faithful. Versatile and adaptable, she takes on life with enthusiasm and a positive attitude.

AADARSHINI [ah-DAHR-shee-nee]

Tamil by origin, Aadarshini means "idealistic." Her idealism is inspirational. She exudes grace and charm. Her friendly and outgoing personality along with her optimistic attitude draws people in. Aadashini is kindhearted and compassionate. She possesses great qualities of a leader.

AADHILA [AHD-hee-lah]

This name means "honesty." Aadhila is a girl who won't lie. She brings beauty to the world with her inspired creativity and artistry. She can be described as charitable and a promoter of peace. Her easygoing personality is loved by all. She is a kind heart. With compassion and understanding, she gives with a generous heart. To her loved ones, she is caring and protective.

AADHIRAI [AHD-hee-ray]

Tamil by origin, Aadhirai refers to "a special star." She glows like a star with her attractiveness and creativity. Her passion and inspiration shine through. She is bright with genuine love and concern for others. She strives for peace and harmony.

AADRITA [AHD-ree-tah]

Indian by origin, Aadrita is synonymous to adorable and charming. The name also signifies one with lots of love to give. Aadrita is indeed a charmer with her romantic, outgoing and friendly persona. She is highly creative and artistic. With a huge heart, she lives her life with kindness, compassion and generosity.

AAGARNA [ah-GAHR-nah]

This Hindu name is synonymous to music or "one who has the gift of music." With an attractive personality, Aagarna draws people in. Her creativity is admirable. She strives for perfection. She is practical and responsible. She has excellent organization skills. She deals with people and life guided by sincerity and honesty.

AALAYA [AH-lah-yah]

In Sanskrit, Aalaya means "home or refuge." She is attracted to the excitement that adventures bring. She enjoys the freedom and lives her life to the fullest. A leader in her own right, Aalaya is responsible, reliable, dynamic, practical and inspiring. She follows a purpose and she acts with immense motivation.

AAMAYA [AH-mah-yah]

Bengali by origin, this name refers to "the pleasant night rain that brings new hope." Aamaya is the calmness after a storm. Loving and caring, she is most genuine. She is remarkable in her skills of the organization. She is practical in dealing with matters. She is always reliable. Her honesty and sincerity are inspiring.

AAMUKTA MALYA [ah-MOOKH-tuh MAHL-yah]

This Hindu name is taken from a poem which is authored by an Indian king named, Sri Krishna Deva Raya. Aamukta Malya has a sense of responsibility. She is consistent and reliable in her words and actions. She likes to lead and supervise. Her confidence may be intimidating but she means well. With great optimism and natural enthusiasm, she inspires others to be the best they can be.

AARINI [AH-ree-nee]

Bengali by origin, Aarini means "someone who is adventurous." Attractive and athletic, she is passionate about like. True to her adventurous spirit, she enjoys exploring and traveling. Rather than resisting, she is one who embraces change. She acts with devotion and genuine concern for others. She finds fulfillment in being able to contribute to the improvement of others.

AARAVI [ah-RAH-vee]

Another Bengali name, Aaravi means "harmony" or a "state of tranquility." She finds inner peace and harmony by teaching others. A consistent and responsible person, Aaravi easily earns the trust of others. She is blessed with creativity. Outgoing and friendly, Aaravi is agreeable and inspirational. She thinks ahead of her time. Her decisions are guided by her vision of her future.

AARADHAYA [ah-RAHD-hah-yah]

This Hindu name means "esteem" and "respect." It also signifies "sentiment of affection." Loving and caring, Aaradhaya puts her loved ones' needs before hers. Being able to care for others gives her a sense of fulfillment.

Armed with a sense of purpose, she is versatile, smart and efficient. She is capable of being a leader. She is a great motivator. She lives a life of example and serves as an inspiration to others. She takes on life with enthusiasm.

ABHISARIKAA [ah-BEE-sah-ree-kah]

In Sanskrit, the name means "beloved one." Among Abhisarikaa's lovable qualities are her diligence, consistency, reliability, practicality and sincerity. She is practical and always thinks about her future. She strives to accomplish her goals. She pushes herself to achieve success and recognition.

ABHITA [ah-BEEh-tah]

This Sanskrit name means "courageous or brave." It refers to someone who is fearless. Indeed, Abhita enjoys her freedom and is not afraid to take risks. She treats life as a series of adventures. She is someone who embraces change and lives her life to the fullest no matter what.

ADISHAKTI [ah-deeh-SHAHK-teeh]

In Sanskrit, Adishakti refers to the "goddess of supreme power." Adishakti embodies this meaning. She exudes confidence, strength and power. She strives hard to accomplish higher goals. She continues to challenge herself.

Adishakti has the strength of character to become a notable leader. She takes initiative and takes control. She is her own person. Her devotion and sympathetic side further add to her admirable qualities.

ANTARA [AHN-tah-rah]

In Sanskrit, Antara refers to the "heart and soul." It signifies that is within. Blessed with wisdom and spirituality, Antara is capable of leading. She is creative and intelligent. She may be introverted but this is what allows her to reflect upon herself and others. She works and acts independently. Although she may seem mysterious, Antara is social, outgoing and friendly.

CHANKRISNA [chahn-KREESH-nah]

This Hindu name refers to a "sweet-smelling tree." Creative, romantic and artistic, Chankrisna possesses many great qualities she can be proud of. With her sympathetic persona, she is a natural peacemaker. To her loved ones, she is devoted, faithful and protective. She is easy-going and understanding. Chankrisna is a hardworking individual who has clear goals for herself. She acts compassionately towards others.

DHARMI [DAHR-meeh]

In Sanskrit, Dharmi refers to one "who is religious." She embodies wisdom and spirituality. She has a deep understanding of people. Intelligent but introverted, she exudes an air of mystery. She is independent and a natural-born leader. She is in full control of her fate.

EKISHA [ey-KEEH-shah]

Indian by origin, this is the name of a Hindu goddess. Ekisha reflects a warm and serene persona. She is genuine in her relationships. Her unpretentious and friendly character draw people in. Patient and understanding, she strives to achieve success. Her family takes her top priority. She is generous to the point of self-sacrificing. She is inclined towards the arts.

HASRI [HAHS-ree]

In Sanskrit, Hasri refers to someone who is "always joyful or happy." She brings joy to those around her with her grace and charm. She acts with compassion. She has a kind heart.

Born with leadership skills, Hasri is intelligent and skillful. She is independent. She likes to be in control.

INIYA [ee-NEE-yah]

This Hindu name means "sweet." Iniya is an attractive person. She takes her responsibilities seriously. In control and independent, she possesses the marks of a capable leader.

KANNITHA [kahn-NEET-huh]

This Hindu name traces its origin from Cambodia and Sanskrit. It means "angels." Angelic in appearance and personality, Kannitha is genuinely loving and caring. She brings peace and harmony by helping others. She is trustworthy. A natural peacemaker, she strives to bridge gaps that separate people. She is devoted and sympathetic. With her many great qualities, she is likely to play an important role in her community.

MONISHA [mow-NEE-shah]

Indian by origin, Monisha refers to someone who is "brilliant, wise and well-learned." She is destined to share her wisdom by teaching others. Her idealism is inspiring and she is bound to lead. Monisha's charm and grace attract people. Her kind and compassionate heart is well admired.

PADMINI [PAHD-mee-nee]

This Hindu name refers to a "multitude of lotuses" or "someone who resides in a lotus." It is also among the various names of the goddess Lakshmi.

Padmini is real and unpretentious. She exudes a warm and friendly nature. She is patient and understanding but also independent. She dreams of taking the lead.

Padmini has a positive outlook on life. She has incredible enthusiasm. With this, she is capable of helping people become the best versions of themselves.

SAARYA [SARH-yuh]

This Hindu name refers to someone who lives in piety. Pious in her ways, Saarya exudes a strong and powerful character at the same time. She is confident about herself and her abilities. She challenges herself to achieve higher goals. Creative and inspirational, Saarya's unique gifts allow her to make a significant impact on other people's lives.

SRAVANTI [SHRA-vahn-tee]

Indian by origin, this Hindu name refers to someone "who flows like a river." Fluid and attractive, Sravanti allows creativity to flow through her veins. She feels the excitement in a rush of adventures. She tends to live her life to the fullest.

YASHICA [yah-SHEE-kuh]

In Sanskrit, Yahica refers to someone who is "intelligent, brave and successful." Smart, independent and bold, Yashica is capable many great things. Her deep sense of purpose is inspiring. She has remarkable enthusiasm. She always looks at the glass half full.

Chapter 7

Traditional names that never fade

Traditional names are names that are dedicated, strong and have a long history and tradition behind them. Many times, they are passed down through the generations from father to son or daughter and have sustained their popularity despite the passage of years. They tend to maintain their appeal from generation to generation and they will remain commonly used by young parents in any given year. Many traditional names are biblical in origin, and many of these names have been used by royalty and others in high office or in history books. Make your choice and don't worry about his name going out of style.

Adam	Graham
Abigail	Ivy
Andrew	Isaac
Andrea	Jean
Garret	John
Anna	Lydia
Thomas	Lucas
Bethany	Maria
William	Mark
Caroline	Nicole
Charles	Matthew
Delia	Phoebe
Darren	Michael
Eliza	Rebecca
David	Philip
Felicia	Sarah
Edward	Richard
Gabrielle	Valerie
Eric	Samuel
Hope	Samantha

Chapter 8

FAQs

Here are some of the most asked questions from parents who are in the process of choosing a name for their baby.

1. My partner and I disagree with names, what do we do?

This scenario is extremely common. You and your partner are different people with different opinions. Baby-names are like flavors of ice cream. Everyone is different. The best situation is if you both compromise and find a middle ground.

In order to do this, sit your partner down and you should both write a list of three names which you like. When you've done this, hand your list to your partner and take theirs. You both have to cross out two names. The name that remains on both lists will be your final two names.

From there, you both have to have a conversation about the name choice. Come to a mutual decision. If you still can't come to an understanding because one of you is not okay with the names they chose, then sit down with this book and go through names again. There is bound to be at least one name you can both agree on.

2. Is it okay to choose a masculine name for my daughter/ a feminine name for my son?

Absolutely! You're the parent and you decide. I've met many Leslies who are men and many Joes who are women. Of course you have to consider the social impact doing this will have on your baby. While there is nothing wrong with naming your son 'Emily', be aware of the impact that will have on your son's life. While it sounds harsh, many kids who are named unisex and opposite sex names are more likely to be taunted or bullied at school.

3. Can I make up a name for my baby?

Yes. Again, you have to be very careful with how you go about this. Making up a name based on another name is 100% fine but naming a child a word which out of context would be misinterpreted is not a good idea. Here are some examples of what is appropriate and what is not. The following are real names which people have named their babies.

Appropriate:	Inappropriate:
- Fox	- Bus
- Leather	- Cup
- Woolf	- Tea-Leaf
- Meclan	- Tackle

You have to make the responsible decision if you have a name in mind which isn't usual.

4. Can I use an alternate spelling for my baby's name?

Of course. In fact, this is encouraged in a lot of cases because alternate spellings can make for some of the most original and beautiful names in the world. For example:

- Adrienn instead of Adrien

- Melisha instead of Melissa

- Franceen instead of Francine

- Lili instead of Lily

Once more, responsibility is key. Not going overboard is a principal aspect of using alternate spellings for baby names.

5. Can I call my baby a name from a different culture to my own?

Can you? Yes.

Should you? It depends.

There are times when doing this could be misconstrued as offensive if you aren't 100% sure of the meaning of a name in another language. In 2012, a man famously made it onto the local newspapers in the South of England because he named his daughter a Chinese name without properly researching the etymology and meaning of the name. It turns out he called her 'Loud Peanut' which is funny but unfortunate.

If you admire a certain culture or language and do the right research behind an ethnic/cultural name, then it would be a lovely tribute to name your child in that language.

6. Can I name my child after myself?

Yes. This is actually called 'juniorising'. Juniorising is where you name your child after his/her father or mother. The name 'jr' (abbreviation of 'junior') follows after his/her name to show this.

There are several categories of names that should generally be avoided. Names of inanimate objects, "way-out" names, names of notorious people, names that too readily lend themselves to ridicule, names which suggest questionable qualities or set inappropriate expectations, and intentional jokes.

The names provided in this list may be taken as negative examples. Many of them are real names that parents have, unfortunately, foisted upon their real children. Some are rumored names, unverified. Finally, some are just posited as examples.

Although another subject, too, really falls under the category of names lending themselves to ridicule, there are unfortunately, as mentioned earlier in this book, some surnames which have taken on meanings or implications over the years, usually through no fault of the family involved, which may be viewed as detrimental to a child. In these cases, parents may want to consider a replacement or alteration to the surname. This is highly personal, and it may be argued that a family legacy is of greater importance than dispersions placed upon it by society; that a child will develop a strong and loyal character by learning to own the name proudly; and even that such a change for the child opens up a whole new problem: Should the parents, too, change their names in order to keep the surnames of the child's family consistent? But it may also be argued that a minor change to the name is a valid means of righting a wrong committed against a family name. Throughout history, such name changes happen all the time. And, if at some time in the future the cultural context changes and the name is no longer a problem, families have been known to revert to the earlier form of the name.

At the end of this section is provided a list of names identified through research that are thought to fall into this category. The reason for the "blacklisting" of these names will be left to the reader's own research, if necessary. For those who do not have such a name, note that we should make every effort to preserve the dignity of persons who have, through no fault of their own, names with such unfortunate associations. For some of those who do, a change is suggested, just as an example of what might be done to remedy the situation.

Names of inanimate objects / brand names

Man-made objects:Banjo

Chevy

Rocket

Marathon

Poncho

Chandelier

Jumper

Food/drink:Wasabi

Caviar

Farro

Cappuccino

Whiskey

Champagne

Chardonnay

Anatomical:Ileum

Jejunum

Ulna

Uvula

Elemental:Silicon

Xenon

Pharmaceutical:Lyrica (Unfortunately, many sounds like names)

Cialis

Viagra

Sanctura

Harvoni

Chantix

"Way-out" names

Space Names:Asteroid

Xanixar

Quasar

Rocket

Flowerchild Names:Blue Ivy

November Rain

Moon Unit

Thyme

Every Man

Earth, Wind, and Fire

Penny Lane

Fairy Tale Names:Leprechaun

SeaMonkey

Pharoah

Out of Era Names:Methuselah - Very subjective; fine names, but maybe not for today.

Ethel

Bobby Sue

Minnie Pearl

Helga

Ursula

Creative:Shaqueque

Doowop Doowop

Taffetiara

Chaneliah

Ja'Lexandera

Unique Brands:CocaCola

Honda

Acura

Mustang

Eno

Chaco

Ajax

Names of notorious people/characters or places

Negatively Notorious:Nixon

Jim Jones

Judas

Lot

Sodom

Gomorrah

Korah

Eve (original sin) - perhaps choose a variation?

Adam (original sin) - perhaps choose a variation?

Jezebel

Pilate

Saul

Herod

Lucifer / Belial

Ananias / Sapphira

Sadaam

Adolf and Hitler

Idi and Amin

Muammar and Gaddafi

Stalin

Osama

Anakin

Darth

Gotham

Hades

Sheol

Alkatraz

Pop Idol:Elton John

(Especially if questionable character)Michael Jackson

Taylor Swift

Justin Bieber

Kardashian

Madonna

Britney

GaGa

Miley

Bowie

Prince

Elvis Pressley

Jenner

Current Political:Obama

Clinton

Trump

Mythology: (Know the character)Oedipus

Zeus

Cronus

Hera

Hades

Athena

Medea

Antaeus

Menos

Ixion

Tantalus

Tragic Victims:Tamar

Bathsheba

Uriah

Dinah

Jonbenet

Pariah

Absolom

Romeo

Juliet (perhaps this one can be overcome with positive attributes)

Names that Lend themselves easily to ridicule:

Negatively suggestive:

Richard (Dick)

Dorcas - sounds like "Dork"

Stonie - sounds like someone who is frequently "stoned"

Dolton - sounds like "Dolt"

Maximus - suggests "gluteus maximus"

Carrien - sounds like "carrion"

Messer - sounds like "mess"

Urina - sounds like "uriine"

Uranus - sounds like "anus"

Fanny

Pet Names:Rover - This group sound like dog's names

Bowser

Trixie

Boomer

Fido

Lala - This group sound like baby names

BooBoo

Baby

Peaches

Honey

Sugar

Lamb

Lollipop

Bunny

Bubba

Princess

Junior

Kitty

Missy

NayNay / NaeNae

Sissy

Queenie

Sweetie

Jokes:

Rhyming Adjective:Lexy or Lexie - "sexy"

Patty - "fatty"

Sounds Like:Ima - sounds like "I'm a..."

Yura, Ura - sounds like "You're a"

Sets:Ping and Pong

Ying and Yang

Elmo, Kermit, and Grover

Larry and Bob

Mind-Altering Drugs Or antidepressants:

Marijuana - No. Even if you are a fan.

Xanax

Cymbalta

Savella

Mercenary TMI:Deduction

Honeymoon

Surprise

Champagne

Cancun

Ritz Carlton

Names which suggest questionable qualities or set unreasonable expectations:

Note: The first group lists two names which are commonly given. These names have so many positive attributes that they generally overcome their original meanings through legacy. Still, it is important to check out possible meanings of a name if you do not already know them. I would be more likely to choose Mary than Mara, because, at least in my culture and experience, it has a better-known legacy, and Emily than Emlin for the same reason.

Negative character?Mary - bitter

Mara - bitter

Emily - rival

Emlin - rival

Nemesis

Rowdy

Rogue

Bruiser

Rage

Fox

Stompie

Chaos

Rebel

Rambo

Carnivores:Tiger

Panther

Cougar

Python

Cobra

Suggestive of impropriety?:Romeo

Shady

Dream

Fantasy

Hustler

Floozy

Free

Lingerie

Cayenne

Abandon

Inappropriate expectations:Beauty

Barbie

Champ

Hercules

Unfortunate Surnames for which a variant might be considered:

Note: In every case but one (Shyster), suggestions are based first upon the intended meaning of the name. In that one exception, suggestions are loosely related or are "sounds-similar" words that do not appear to have such negative meanings. Possible adjustments to other "problem" names might be approached in the same way.

Hooker (Hook maker) - Hooke, Hookmaker, Hookmacher?

Dick (Short for Richard) - Richards, Richard?

Seaman (Sea Man) - Seaworth, Seaworthy, Seafarer, Seaside?

Gay (Glad) - Glad, Gladd, Glade?

Gayward (Glad-like) - Gladward, Gladdward?

Butts (Bulls-eye, Target) - Archer, Arrow, Aim, Aims, Aimes?

Fuchs (Fox), Fucks, Fucksman, Focker - Fox, Fox, Foxman, Foxman, Foxer?

Virgin - Virgo, Virge, Virtue?

Manlove - Loveman, Loveman, Mann, Love?

Dicker (Dyke worker/builder) - Dyker, Diggar, Digman, Dykeman?

Frick (Smith) - Fevre, Feaver, Smith?

Heine (Home rule) - Henrich, Hendrich, Henrick, Hendry, Henric?

Roach (Rock) - Rock, Stone, Rockman, Stoneman

Pot (Pit) - Phillips, Pitt, Pittman

Schmuck (Jeweller or Neat and tidy) - Jeweller, Bright, Order?

Shyster (Ohboy... let's just make up something!) - Lawman, Lawman, Schist, Christ?

Messer (Hayward, one responsible for gathering/keeping hay) - Hayer, Hayman, Hay?

Raper (Rope maker) - Roper, Ropere, Ropemaker, Rope?

Gasser (Road or Alley resident) - Alley, Streeter, Street, Lane?

Loser - (Lazarus/Eleazer/Elieser) - Lazar, Eleazer, Elieser, Eli?

Klutz (Clumsy) - Tripp (Existing name that means the same thing, but sounds better.)?

Fly (Flageum / Flavius) - Flyer, Flyman, Flymann?

Slaughter (various) - Sloh, Slough, Sloetree?

Boner (de bonne aire) - Bonnaire, Bonaire, Bonne?

Chapter 9

Famous Names

Popular Names from Politicians and Influential People

Some people like to name their children after presidents and influential people.

So if you are passionate about politics, this list may help narrow down your choices. Nothing grand here. Remember, plain works. Feel free to use a variation of the names as well, these are just here to give you a few more ideas!

Names of Presidents for Boys

George Washington

James Monroe

William Henry

James Garfield

Franklin Pierce

John Adams

James Madison

Theodore Roosevelt

Calvin Coolidge

James Buchanan

Andrew Johnson

Ulysses Grant

John Quincy Adams

Thomas Jefferson

Martin Van Buren

John Tyler

Zachary Taylor

Millard Fillmore

Rutherford Hayes

Chester Arthur

James Polk

William McKinley

William Taft

Benjamin Harrison

Warren Harding

Ronald Reagan

Bill Clinton

George Bush

Barack Obama

Other Notable Politicians

Moon Landrieu – Secretary of Housing and Urban Development

Oveta Culp Hobby – Secretary of Health, Education and Welfare

Alben Barkley – Vice President under Harry Truman

Schuyler Colfax – Vice President under Ulysses Grant

Danforth Quayle – Vice President under George Bush

Famous Names of Writers and Artists

If you adore Shakespeare, Agatha Christie, and Maya Angelou among others, you might consider naming your child after one of the people listed below.

Boy's Names

Gabriel Garcia

Herman Melville

Nathaniel Hawthorne

Walt Whitman

Gustave Klimt

David Hockney

Geoffrey Chaucer

Salvador Dali

Girl's Names

Alice Walker

Agatha Christie

Frida Kahlo

Georgia O' Keeffe

Jane Austen

Nora Ephron

Gloria Steinem

Famous Rock and Roll Names

Boy's Names

Elton John

Freddie Mercury

Jimmy Buffett

John Lennon

Paul McCartney

Robert Palmer

David Lee Roth

Kurt Cobain

Bruce Springsteen

Girl's Names

Alanis Morrissett

Annie Lennox

Janis Joplin

Tina Turner

Melissa Etheridge

Alison Moyet

Popular Celebrity Names

Boy's Names

Andy Garcia

Antonio Banderas

Brad Pitt

Christopher Reeves

Dennis Quaid

Eddie Murphy

Clint Eastwood

Harry Hamlin

Dean Cain

Harvey Keitel

James Dean

Jimmy Stewart

Lenny Bruce

Macaulay Culkin

Ralph Macchio

Mel Gibson

Matt Dillon

Sammy Davis

Steven Seagal

Wesley Snipes

William Baldwin

Girl's Names

Alicia Silverstone

Angela Bassett

Bette Davis Demi Moore

Glenn Close

Goldie Hawn

Meryl Streep

Michelle Pfeiffer

Sharon Stone

Angelina Jolie

Julia Roberts

Emma Thompson

Gilda Radner

Halle Berry

Jennifer Lawrence

Sandra Bullock

Sharon Stone

Selina Gomez

Vanessa Hudgens

Winona Ryder

What Famous Celebrities are Naming their Babies

Americans adore celebrities and this fact can't help but be mirrored in the names given to kids. Not only do parents name their kids after their Hollywood idols, but they also go out of their way naming them after the kids that the stars are having.

For Girls

Claudia Rose – daughter of Michelle Pfeiffer

Zoe – daughter of Amanda Bearse

Sasha – daughter of Steven Spielberg

Annie – daughter of Jamie Lee Curtis

Molly – daughter of Terri Garr

Tara – daughter of Oliver Stone

Danielle – daughter of Jerry Lewis

Renee – daughter of Rod Stewart

Matalin Mary – daughter of Mary Matalin

For Boys

Nicolas – son of Jean-Claude Van Damme

Jett – son of Jon Travolta

Cody – son of Robin Williams

Jack Henry - son of Meg Ryan

Alexander James - son of Andy Mill

Christian Aurelia - son of Arnold Schwarzenegger

Michael Garrett – son of Melissa Gilbert

Famous Country Music Names

Country music is a big hit. This is precisely the reason why many parents would love to have their babies named after their favorite country music singer.

Boy's names

Chet Atkins

Garth Brooks

George Jones

Kenny Rogers

Waylon Jennings

Lee Clayton

Girl's Names

Crystal Gayle

Loretta Lynn

Taylor Swift

Shania Twain

Wynonna Judd

Dolly Parton

Naomi Judd

Reba McEntire

Patty Lovelace

Chapter 10

Biblical Names and Meanings

In this chapter, I have a list of names from the bible along with a brief description of that person's role in the book and a description of the origins of the name. As you will see, the majority, but not all, of these names have origins in the Hebrew language.

Key – Name – boy's name

Name – girl's name

Name – gender-neutral name

A

Aaron – (role in the bible) the brother of Moses – (meaning) it's Hebrew origins mean a teacher, or a high mountain, metaphorically a mountain of strength or wisdom.

Abda – a servant of Solomon – it originates from the Arabic for extraordinary, or beautiful.

Abdeel – the father of Shelemiah – a Hebrew word meaning a cloud from God, or a servant to God

Abigail – sister of David – from the Hebrew meaning the joy of the father.

Abraham – father to Isaac – a Hebrew name which means father to the multitude.

Adah – a wife of Lamech – a Hebrew name meaning adornment.

Adam – first man, in the Garden of Eden – this is the Hebrew word for man.

Adina – a mighty member of the army of David – it means slender one, and is from Hebrew.

Ahab – a king of Israel – uncle, or father's brother, from Hebrew.

Aisha – a senior member of the household of Solomon – the brother of a prince, from Hebrew.

Ajah – Son of Ezer – an old English name, which means a goat, sometimes a hawk.

Amos – an ancestor of Jesus – the name is from Hebrew and means borne by God.

Amzi – an Israelite exile – strong or one's own strength. Although the name is biblical, and is therefore probably of Hebrew origin, it is uncertain from where the name originated.

Anah – a daughter of Zibeon and a son of Seir – a discoverer or explorer; one who finds the answer. The name is from Hebrew.

Anaiah – a supporter of Ezra – an answer to God – the Hebrew name was originally a boy's name but of late it has become more popular for girls.

Andrew – an Apostle of Jesus Christ – a word derived from Greek, and which means manly.

Anna – a prophet – originally from Latin, it means given grace or favor.

Arah – son of Ulla – a traveler or wayfarer, the name is of indeterminate origin, and can be applied for boys or girls.

Asher – a son of Jacob – from Hebrew origins, it means happiness.

Azzan – the father of a prince – from Hebrew, it means strong.

B

Barkos – the father to the Nethinim – most probably this means a painter, but its entomology is uncertain.

Barnabus – a minor apostle – an Aramaic word, which means consolation.

Bartholomew – an Apostle of Jesus Christ – another name with Aramaic origins, it means a son.

Basemath – wife of Esau – sweet-smelling or sweet of smile, it is a Hebrew word.

Ben Dekar – one of Solomon's main administrators – a son (of Pick), this is a name with Hebrew origins.

Benjamin - a son of Jacob – a Hebrew word, and as a name often given to the youngest son. It means right-hand son.

C

Caleb – son of Hezron – a Hebrew name which means one who is bold.

Candace (Candice) – an Ethiopian Queen who found God – this is from Latin, and means purity or whiteness.

Carshena (Karshena) – A high ranking official in the court of King

Ahasuerus – wolf-like or wolfish for a boy, lamb-like for a girl. The derivation of the name is unknown.

Chalcol – a man almost as wise as Solomon – steady or reliable. This is from the Hebrew language.

Claudia – an associate of the Apostle Paul – the name is from the Latin for lame.

D

Dalphon – a son of Haman – from the Hebrew to weep

Dan - a son of Jacob – a Hebrew name which means God is my judge.

Daniel – savior of Susanna, who had been falsely accused of adultery – the full form of Dan (above)

Deborah – a nursemaid – it is the Hebrew for a bee.

Delilah – the love of Samson – this is also a Hebrew name, and it means lovelorn, and also seductive.

Dodo – a hero from Bethlehem – beloved, or father's brother this is from Hebrew.

E

Elasah – a descendent of Saul – a Hebrew word meaning made by God

Eli – a priest – a name descended from Greek, and meaning a defender of man.

Elijah – a prophet – a Hebrew name which means Jehovah is God, or God the lord.

151

Eliphalet or Eliphelet – one of the sons of David (note, there are several spelling variations for this name) – it comes from the Hebrew for God delivers.

Elisheba – The sister in law of Moses, and wife of Aaron – God is my oath is the meaning of this name, which is a Hebrew term.

Elnathan (much more commonly known as Nathan) – the father of Nehushta – a Hebrew term which means given by God

Elon – a judge of Israel – it refers to an oak tree in Hebrew.

Enoch – the first son of Cain – it is a Hebrew name which means dedicated.

Eri – a son of Gad – watchful or careful; a Hebrew name.

Eve – the first woman, in the Garden of Eden – it is a Latin word which means life.

G

Gad - a son of Jacob – possibly a Hebrew word for the Juniper tree, or a Scandinavian term meaning to cut, or invade.

Gamul (more usually chosen in the form of Samuel) – an important priest – a rewarded one, one whom God has heard. It is a Hebrew name.

Gideon – the son of Joash – a Hebrew name that means a hewer, or one who cuts down.

H

Hakkatan – the father of Johanan, and leader of a line of descendants from Ezra – the small one, or simply small, it is from the Hebrew for being small.

Hannah – a person of Jerusalem, and a prophet – it is from the Hebrew, and means favor or grace.

I

Ira – the priest of David – it comes from the Latin for wrath.

Isaac – son of Abraham - it is from the Hebrew for laughter.

Issachar - a son of Jacob – a Hebrew word which comes to mean 'his reward will come'.

Iscah (also Jesca, Yiscah and most commonly Jessica) – the daughter of Haran and sister of Lot – a name with Hebrew origins, it means watchful

J

James – a brother of Jesus – a Latin term, with links to Greek and Hebrew, which means one who supplants another.

Jamin (also, Benjamin) – one of the sons of Simeon – right-hand man, a Hebrew form.

Jareb – a king of Assyria – a Hebrew word for a great king, although it might specifically relate to an epithet for an Assyrian king.

Jemima – a daughter of Job – a Hebrew word meaning a dove

Joanna – helped to prepare the body of Jesus for burial – from the Greek meaning God is gracious.

Jochebed – the mother of Moses – a Hebrew term meaning God's glory.

Joel – the eldest son of Samuel, a prophet – a Hebrew name which means one who commands.

John – an Apostle of Jesus Christ – another Hebrew name which means that God has been gracious.

Jonathan – a survivor of the destruction of Jerusalem – being another version of John, its origins are also Hebrew, and the meaning is similar to John, in this case, God-given

Joseph – the father of Jesus, and a son of Jacob – a Hebrew name is meaning increased by God.

Joshua – the owner of the field where the Ark finally came to rest – From the Hebrew, meaning God saves, there are links through the Latin Iesus, which means Jesus in English.

Judith – wife of Esau – a Hebrew name meaning a woman of Judea.

Judah - a son of Jacob – meaning one who is praised, the name is derived from Hebrew.

Jude – a brother of Jesus – a different version of Judah, this is from Greek, but has the same meaning as Judah.

Julia – a Christian woman of Rome – the female equivalent to Julius, the name is from Latin and means young.

Junia - a person respected by St Paul – another version of Julia and Julius, it can be for both boys and girls, and comes from the Latin meaning young.

K

Keren – one of Job's daughters – a Hebrew name which means glorious dignity.

Keziah (sometimes Kezia or Cassia) – the second daughter of the Job – a Hebrew name meaning smelling of sweet-scented spice.

L

Lael – the father of Eliasaph – a Hebrew, gender-neutral name meaning belonging to God

Lazarus – a believer in Jesus Christ – a Hebrew name meaning helped by God.

Leah – the first wife of Jacob – a Hebrew name is meaning weary.

Levi - a son of Jacob – a Hebrew name which means an ally, or friend.

Linus - one of the associates of Paul, the Apostle – a Greek name, which translates to fair or flaxen-haired.

Lois (more often Louise) – St Timothy's grandmother - A name of Greek origins, it means superior.

Luke – a believer in Jesus Christ – from the Latin meaning light.

Lydia – an early convert to Christianity – a Greek name, meaning a beautiful or noble one.

M

Mahalath – a wife of Esau – a Hebrew name meaning a tender one.

Malchiel – the grandson of Asher – a Hebrew name meaning my God is my King

Mark – a believer in Jesus Christ – a Latin name meaning a hammer, or a warrior.

Martha – a believer in Jesus Christ – an Aramaic name, which means the mistress of the house.

Mary – mother of Jesus Christ – a Latin name which means star of the sea.

Matthew – an Apostle of Jesus Christ – a Hebrew name meaning a gift from God.

Matthias – a minor apostle – also meaning a gift from God, it is similar to Matthew, but also has Greek origins.

Mehetable or Mehitable – the wife of Hadad – made good by God, most probably from Hebrew.

Melea – the father of Eliakim – in the genealogy of God; probably from Greek.

Merab – in the bible, a daughter of Saul, this name is also used for boys – it is from Hebrew, and means abundant.

Michael – a member of the House of Asher – a Hebrew name which means like God.

Miriam – the sister of Moses – a Hebrew version of Mary, likewise meaning a star of the sea.

N

Naomi – Ruth's mother in law – a Hebrew name is meaning pleasant.

Naphtali - a son of Jacob – a Hebrew variant is meaning a wrestler.

Noah – the man who built the ark, also the daughter of Zelophehad – a Hebrew name meaning consolation. In a biblical context, it could also mean long-lived.

O

Obadiah – one of David's descendants – a Hebrew name meaning servant of the Lord.

Obil – as Ishmaelite – a keeper of animals, especially camels. A shepherd when used for boys, or one who weeps for the weepers, more often for girls. It is a Hebrew name.

Onesimus – a believer in Jesus Christ – a Latin name for one who will be profitable.

Orpah – the sister in law of Ruth – a Moabite name is meaning a fawn.

P

Paul – a minor apostle – from the Latin meaning small.

Peter – an apostle of Jesus – from the Latin meaning a rock

Philemon (Philomena) – a believer in Jesus Christ – a Greek name, meaning one who kisses.

Phoebe – a deaconess – from the Greek for a shining one.

Priscilla – a believer in Jesus Christ – from the Latin for venerable.

R

Rachel – Jacob's second wife – a Hebrew name is meaning lamb.

Rapha (a form of Raphael) – a parent of Jessi – from the Hebrew meaning the healing powers of God.

Repeal (another form of Raphael) – a son of Shemaiah – the same meaning as Rapha.

Reuben - a son of Jacob – this is from Hebrew for who sees the son?

Ruth – the wife of Boaz – a Hebrew name, meaning friend.

S

Salome – daughter of Herodias – a Hebrew name, meaning peace

Saph – an enemy of David – a Hebrew name meaning giant, or from a family of giants

Sarah – the wife of Abraham, and Isaac's mother – from the Hebrew meaning princess.

Silas – a believer in Jesus Christ – a word from the Greek, which means woods or forest.

Simeon - a son of Jacob – it is a Hebrew term, meaning a listener.

Simon – an Apostle of Jesus Christ – A Greek name with a slightly different meaning to Simeon above, Simon means heard by God.

Stephen – the first martyr – a Greek name which means a crown or wreath.

Susanna – a victim of false accusations, saved by Daniel – a Hebrew name meaning lily.

T

Tabitha – a doer of good and aid to the poor – a person who is graceful. It is from Greek origins, although has links to Hebrew and Aramaic, where it means a gazelle.

Tamar (more often, Tamara) – a daughter of David – the name is from the Hebrew, and means a date palm.

Tapath (a variant of Tabitha) – a daughter of Solomon – see Tabitha above.

Timothy – a believer in Jesus Christ – from the Greek, and means to honor God.

Titus – a believer in Jesus Christ – in this context, from the Latin for saved. It also has Green connotations, where it means a giant.

U

Uri (from Uriah) – a member of the Judah tribe – my flame, or my light from Hebrew.

Uriah – a prophet – see Uriah above.

V

Vanish (Vania for girls) – one of the sons of Bani – In this context it is from the Hebrew meaning nourishment of the Lord, or gift to God. It has a Latin background also, where the meaning is slightly different, being a bringer of good news.

Z

Zabud - a priest and friend of King Solomon – endowed, most probably from Hebrew origins.

Zebediah (also Zebedee) – a son of Ishmael - given by good, from the Hebrew.

Zebulun - a son of Jacob – from the Ugaritic (Ugarit is a coastal part of Syria) for a prince.

Zephon – a son of Gad – a Hebrew name which means an angel, or one who expects good.

Chapter 11

Names Based on Locations

A name stemming from a location can have personal meaning, such as where the parents' wedding took place, or even where their baby was born. Or, it can simply be chosen because of the beautiful phonetic sounds these names have.

Girls

Adelaide - City in Australia - German

Africa - Continent - Latin

Albany- white, fair" - the capital of New York - Latin

Alberta - Province in Canada - Anglo-Saxon

Alexandria - City in Virginia, USA - Greek

America - Country in North America - Latin

Andorra - European Principality in Eastern Pyrenees mountains - English

Arabia - "Desert, Evening, Ravens," - Saudi Arabia in Asia - Biblical

Arizona - "little springs" - state in USA - Native American

Asia- Means "east," Continent - Greek

Aspen - City in Colorado, USA - English

Atlanta - City in Georgia, USA - Greek/Latin

Austin - means "Majestic dignity," - a city in Texas, USA - Latin

Avalon - "island of apples" - City in California, USA - Celtic

Bailey - Means "able," - a city in Colorado, USA - German

Berlin - "river rake" or "bear" - City in Germany, German

Bethany - "house of figs" - Village outside of Jerusalem in Bible - Biblical/Hebrew

Bolivia - Country in South America; Spanish

Boston - City in Massachusetts, USA; English

Brazil - Country in South America, Portuguese

Brittany - Region in France; English/Celtic

Brooklyn - "stream" - City in NY, USA - English

Cairo - "the victorious" - City in Egypt - Arabic

Calais - City in France 3 hrs from Paris - French

Canada - "villiage" - Country in North America - Iroquois

Carolina - "Strong" - States North and South Carolina, USA - Latin

Catalina - "Pure" - Santa Catalina Island (California), Spanish

Charlotte - "free man" - City in North Carolina, USA - French

Chelsea - "seaport" - District of London, England; English

Cheyenne - City and capital of Wyoming; Native American

China - "Qin's kingdom" - a country in Asia; English

Dakota - "friend" - states North and South Dakota, USA - Native American; Sioux

Devon - "defender" - County in England - Gaelic

Dijon - City in France - French

Dixie - "tenth" - an old, generic term for the southern states of USA- Latin

Eden - "paradise" - Biblical location (ie: garden of paradise) - Hebrew

Egypt - Country in N. Africa - (origin debated: Ancient Egyptian, Greek, and/or Arabic)

Everest - tallest mountain in the world - Nepal and China - English

Fatima - City in Portugal - Portuguese

Florence - "blooming" - a city in Tuscany, Italy - Latin

Florida - "flourishing" - State in USA - Latin

France - "French" - Country in Europe - English

Gaza - the largest city in Palestine - Arabic

Geneva- "estuary" or "race of women" or "juniper"- a city in Switzerland - Latin/French

Genoa - city in Italy - Latin

Georgia - "earth-worker" - State in USA - English

Havana - "beauty" - the capital city of Cuba - Spanish

Haven - "safe place" - city New Haven, Michigan, USA - English

Heaven - "paradise" - Biblical location of Paradise - English

Helena - "bright, shining light" - city in Montana - Greek

Holland - location in The Netherlands - Dutch

India - Country in South Asia - Latin

Indiana - State in USA - English

Ireland - 3rd largest island in Europe - English

Java - island in Indonesia - English

Jordan - "descending" - kingdom in Asia - Hebrew

Juneau - Capital of Alaska, USA - French

Juno - Town in Texas, USA - English

Kenya - "yes to God" - a country in Africa - Hebrew

Kimberley - "royal fortress, meadow" - a town in Tasmania, Australia - English

Kimberly - "royal fortress, meadow" - a ghost town in Nevada, USA - English

Lisbon - the capital of Portugal - Portuguese

London - Capital of the UK - English

Lorraine - a city in France - French

Lourdes - city in France - Spanish

Lydia - Kingdom in Asia - Greek

Madison - "Madison Square Garden" in Wisconsin, USA - English

Maison- "house" - Maisons-Laffitte - Commune in north-central France - French

Malta - "honey-sweet" - Mediterranean island - Greek

Marina - "man/woman of the sea" - city in California, USA - Latin

Marsala - city in Sicily - Italian

Mecca - City in Saudi Arabia - Arabic

Mercia - Kingdom in Britain - English

Miami - city in Florida - English

Milan - a city in Italy - Italian

Montana - "mountain" - state in USA - Latin

Myrtle - city in Minnesota, USA - Greek

Nevada - "snow-capped" - State in USA - Spanish

Oasis - area of vegetation in the desert - Greek

Odessa - a city in Ukraine - Russian

Panama - "many butterflies" or "an abundance of fish" - region/ republic in Central America - Spanish

Paris - the capital of France - Greek

Persia - Empire (Officially Islamic Republic of Iran) in Asia - Latin

Regina - "queen" - the capital of Saskatchewan, Canada - Latin

Rome - "strength, power" - Capital of Italy - Latin

Russia - the largest country in the world in Eurasia - Greek

Sahara - "dawn, desert" - desert in N. Africa - Arabic

Samaria - "watch mountain, watchtower" - ancient city/capital of Northern Kingdom of Isreal- Latin/Hebrew

Savannah - "treeless plain" - a city in Georgia, USA - Spanish

Seville - "prophetess, oracle" - city in Spain - Spanish

Shannon - "wise river" - river in Ireland - Irish

Sharon - "plain (geographic)" - plain in Palestine - Hebrew

Shasta - "teacher" - volcanic peak in California - English/Sanskrit

Sicily -Island in Mediterranean - Italian

Sierra - "mountain range" - the Sierra Madre in the Philippines on Luzon Island - Spanish

Sonoma - "valley of the moon" - Sonoma Valley County in California - English/Native American

Svea - ancient name for Sweden - Swedish

Sydney - a city in Australia - French

Tulsa - "strength, power" - Capital of Italy - Latin

Valencia - "brave" - a city in Italy - Italian/Latin

Venice - City in Italy - Italian

Venezia - "from the city of Venice" - relation to Venice, Italy - Italian

Verona - City in Italy - Latin

Victoria - "triumphant" - the capital of British Columbia, Canada - Latin

Vienna - "chosen one" - the capital of Austria - German

Virginia - "virgin" - State in USA - Latin

Return to Table of Contents

Boys

Africa - continent - Latin

Albany - "white, fair" - the capital of New York - Latin

Arlington - city in Virginia, USA - English

Arizona - "little springs" - state in USA - Native American

Aspen - city in Colorado - English

Austin - "great, magnificent" - city in Texas, USA - Latin

Bailey - "able" - a city in Colorado - German

Berlin - "river rake" or "bear" -the capital of Germany - German

Brazil - Country in S. America - Portuguese

Bremen - state and city in Germany - German

Brighton - "bright settlement" - a city in England - English

Boston - the capital of Massachusetts, USA - English

Bristol - "bridge location" - a city in England - English

Brooklyn - "stream" - City in NY, USA - English

Bronx - county of New York City, USA - English

Camden - "from the valley" - historic town in New South Whales - Celtic

Carson - City in California, USA - Celtic

Caspian - "The Caspian Sea" between Europe and Asia - English

Chad - "battle, warrior" - a country in Africa - Welch

Chandler - "candle maker" - Island in Antarctica - French

Cody - "helpful" - city in Florida, USA - English

Columbus - the capital of Ohio, USA - English

Cuba - Republic and island in the Caribbean Sea - Spanish

Dakota - "friend" - states North and South Dakota, USA - Native American; Sioux

Dale - "valley" - community in Ontario, Canada - Old English

Dallas - "valley of water" - city in Texas, USA - Irish

Dayton - "dairy town" - city in Ohio, USA - English

Denver - "valley" - a city in Colorado, USA - English

Devon - "defender" - county in England - Irish

Diego - "teacher" - city San Diego, California, USA - Spanish

Dijon - City in France - French

Eugene - "well-born" - county in Oregon, USA - Greek

Everest - largest mountain in the world, Mt. Everest - China and

Nepal - English

Forrest - a river in Kimberley, Australia - Latin

France - "French" - a country in Europe - Latin

Francisco - "San Francisco" city in California, USA - Spanish

Gary - "spear-carrier"- a city in Indiana - English

Glen - "secluded valley" - "Great Glen" large, famous valley in Scotland - Irish/Scottish

Guadalupe - "wolf river" - city in Mexico - Spanish

Hamilton - "beautiful mountain" - City in Ontario, Canada - English

Holland - region in The Netherlands - Dutch

Houston - "hill town" - city in Texas, USA - English

Hudson - "The Hudson River" in NY, USA - English

Indiana - State in USA - English

Indio - "indigenous people" - City in California, USA - Spanish

Ireland - 3rd largest island in Europe - English

Israel - "may God prevail" -Republic in the Middle East - Hebrew

Jackson - the capital of Mississippi, USA - Hebrew

Jerico - "city of the moon" - City in Columbia, South America - Spanish

Jersey - "grassy island" - location in the UK on the coast of Normandy, France - English

Jordan - "descend, flow down" - a kingdom in Western Asia - Hebrew

Kent - "coast" - county in England - Welsh/English

Kingston - "King's field" - the capital of Jamaica - English

Kyle - "channel, strait, handsome" - town in Saskatchewan, Canada - Gaelic

Laredo - city in Texas, USA - Spanish

Lincoln - "lithe" - city in Buenos Aires, Argentina - Latin

London - the capital of the UK - English

Madison - "Madison Square Garden" in Wisconsin, USA - English

Maison - "house" - Maisons-Laffitte - Commune in north-central France - French

Marshall - "horse keeper" - a city in Alaska, USA - French

Melbourne - "mill stream" - the capital of Victoria, Australia - English

Memphis - "enduring, beautiful" - city in Tennessee, USA - Latin/Greek/Egyptian

Mitchell - "big" - Mitchell Island in British Columbia, Canada - Middle English

Montreal - city in Quebec, Canada - French

Orlando - "famous island, famed land" city in Florida, USA - German/Spanish

Oslo - the capital of Norway - Norwegian

Paris - Capital of France - Greek

Peyton - "royal" - location in El Paso County, Colorado, USA - Scottish

Phoenix - "mythical, beautiful bird of rebirth" - city in Arizona, USA - Latin/Greek

Raleigh - "roe deer clearing" - the capital of North Carolina, USA - Old English

Reno - city in Nevada - English

Richmond - "wise protector" - the capital of Virginia, USA - German

Rio - "river" - city Rio de Janeiro in Brazil - Spanish

Rome - "strength, power" - Capital of Italy - Latin

Salem - "peace" - (in Bible) Ancient Jerusalem - Hebrew

Santiago - the capital of Chile - Spanish

Sydney - a city in Australia - French

Texas - "friends, allies" - the state is USA - Spanish

Trenton - "river" - a town in Nova Scotia, Canada - English

Troy - "curly-haired" - ancient city in ruins in Asia Minor - English

Vegas - "meadows" - city Las Vegas in Nevada, USA - Spanish

Washington - "active" - Washington D.C. - the capital of USA - English

York - a city in NE England - English

Zaire - "river that swallows all rivers" - former name of the Democratic Republic of the Congo, Africa - African

Zion - "promised land, eutopia" - hill in Jerusalem - Hebrew

Zurich - a city in Switzerland – German

Conclusion

You're here, you've made it to the end of the book. We sincerely hope that you've benefitted from it. Perhaps you've found your perfect name, or you haven't quite decided yet. Hopefully, you at least have some prospects that you can think about. Our recommendation is to write them down and to think about them for a couple of weeks. Say or shout the names out loud and you will begin to get a feel for the names. Thank you very much for reading this book, we wish you all the best!

Now that you have come to the end of this book, we would first like to express our gratitude for choosing this particular source and taking the time to read through it.

We hope you found it useful and you can now use it as a guide anytime you want. You may also want to recommend it to any family or friends that you think might find it useful as well.

Made in the USA
Coppell, TX
01 February 2020

15228637R10098